I 2/9/12 WLPT        12:99

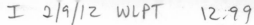
THE NEW MOM'S GUIDE TO
# life with
# baby

THE NEW MOM'S GUIDE TO
# life with baby

## Susan Besze Wallace
### with Monica Reed, MD

Revell

a division of Baker Publishing Group
Grand Rapids, Michigan

© 2009 by MOPS International

Combined edition published 2011

Previously published in four separate volumes:
*The New Mom's Guide to Living on Baby Time*
*The New Mom's Guide to Your Body after Baby*
*The New Mom's Guide to Dealing with Dad*
*The New Mom's Guide to Finding Your Own Mothering Style*

Published by Revell
a division of Baker Publishing Group
P.O. Box 6287, Grand Rapids, MI 49516-6287
www.revellbooks.com

Printed in the United States of America

Library of Congress Cataloging-in-Publication Data
Wallace, Susan Besze, 1969–
    The new mom's guide to life with baby / Susan Besze Wallace, with Monica Reed.
        p.   cm.
    "Previously published in four separate volumes: The New Mom's Guide to Living on Baby Time; The New Mom's Guide to Your Body after Baby; The New Mom's Guide to Dealing with Dad; The New Mom's Guide to Finding Your Own Mothering Style."
    ISBN 978-0-8007-2027-8 (pbk.)
    1. Mothers. 2. Mothers—Family relationships. 3. Mothers—Health and hygiene. 4. Mother and infant. 5. Infants—Care. I. Reed, Monica. II. Title. III. Title: New mom's guide to living on baby time. IV. Title: New mom's guide to dealing with dad. VI. Title: New mom's guide to finding your own mothering style.
HQ759.W3135  2010
649'.122—dc22
                                                                    2010045879

The internet addresses, email addresses and phone numbers in this book are accurate at the time of publication. They are provided as a resource. Baker Publishing Group does not endorse them or vouch for their content or permanence.

The information provided herein should not be construed as prescribed health-care advice or instruction. The information is provided with the understanding that the publisher does not enter into a health-care practitioner/patient relationship with its readers. Readers who rely on information in this publication to replace the advice of health-care professionals, or who fail to consult with health-care professionals, assume all risks of such conduct.

Published in association with the literary agency of Alive Communications, Inc., 7680 Goddard Street, Suite 200, Colorado Springs, CO 80920.

11  12  13  14  15  16  17     7  6  5  4  3  2  1

# Contents

Part 1

# Living on Baby Time

# Introduction

## *My New Center*

I was standing at the kitchen counter, poised to attack the stacks of mail and bills and newspapers and dirty dishtowels surrounding me, and I heard it—my new baby's cry.

*No. Not yet. Not again. I haven't gotten anything done. I haven't even showered. The books said he should nap about two hours.* I tried to will him back to sleep. I even muttered a prayer under my breath. *Pleeeease, not yet. I need to do my stuff.*

He wailed again.

I unclenched my fists and my eyes and made my way to my baby's room.

I'd spent my son's young life trying to deal with him—nourish him, situate him—so I could get back to *my* stuff. I thought that was a mom's routine. But for some reason, on this day, a lightbulb went on, as I felt defeated by the number of things on my to-do list. A voice inside said, *He isn't a thing.* He is *the* thing, my "stuff," my new center. And whatever else I thought was so important to do, that should move to the sidelines for now.

It was a beautiful, pivotal, helpful moment for me as a new mom who thrived, and still thrives, on being productive. Of course that didn't help me write overdue thank-you notes, descudge my floor, or read something more invigorating than the ibuprofen bottle. You get the picture. You are probably living it.

Before kids, you controlled most things—when you ate, when you showered, how long you took to dry your hair, and whether you called in sick to work. Now a baby's rhythms of eating, needing to be held, playing, and sleeping dictate the use of your days—and your nights. You might not have expected motherhood to feel so all-encompassing, so stifling at moments. Even when motherhood feels wonderful, it's overwhelming.

"This too shall pass," my mom always likes to say. But we can *enjoy* the passage of these baby days, not just survive them. And we should. Our children absorb our attitudes—and our stress—from the get-go. Breathe deeply and get ready to take a look inside your mothering so far—what you do and how you feel about it. You always have enough time to be inspired by a new idea for making the most of this very unique season of life.

# 1

## What's Normal

### *Adjusting Your Expectations*

Every morning when I lifted a little body out of a crib, big blue eyes looking to me for direction and nourishment, I felt a stabbing sense of being alone. That was true with my first child, when the only other sound around was the tinkling of a dog collar. It was true with my second, as I started juggling conversations with a preschooler while caring for the baby. And it was true with my third, when there were two other kids romping or eating breakfast while I locked eyes with the baby for the first time that day. I still felt alone.

It wasn't a scary alone, like walking through a haunted house (though cobwebs were increasingly easy to find!). It was more of a heaviness, knowing I was the one who would choose everything that would touch my child's life that day, and most days. I would decide what he would eat and wear and whom he would see. I would choose where he would sleep and what he would hear. With each baby it was at once exciting and overwhelming. The days rolled forward, and the decisions collected like a snowball rolling downhill. Early on I didn't take many opportunities to stop and see what shape the snowball was taking or to pick the twigs out or just to stop rolling once in a while.

The question that pummeled me day after day after day was this: Was I doing it *right*? Millions of women were doing the same thing, but how did *they* do it? Did they dress baby *before* breakfast? Give a bath in the morning or at night? Had they started baby sign language at this age? Did they sleep when the baby did, as the books insisted? Maybe they were already out losing baby bulge by pushing the jogger stroller. Maybe they had nannies and were still in the sack at 9 a.m.

Are you wondering if you're missing something that will make life easier, more enjoyable, and less exhausting? My experience to date says you will always wonder. You should indeed take stock of your routine and strive to do things well, but new moms tend to get whiplash trying to keep up with the volley of advice on raising baby coming their way.

Slow down. Sit down.

For a moment let go of the how-to books, the clock, the thoughts about what other moms are doing. Look squarely at the unique little life that is blessing you. Love that baby. Your days—and all those decisions—will fall into place just fine. You have time to work on the details, but that moment

"You hear it and you hear it: 'Cherish those moments.' But that is truly incredible advice when I look back. I wrote down my son's firsts— when that tooth came in, his first word—but they are just on two sheets of paper in the front of a baby book—a baby book that isn't put together. He's five! I was too busy to cherish the moments.

I think you have to make a conscious decision to focus on those important moments, even if you have to let some things go. Because time will go. I had a friend in elementary school, and all I remember about her house is that her mom was cleaning every single time I was there. I don't want to be that mom."

Vanessa

you just gazed at your baby—that particular moment—is gone forever. You've just been told what millions of moms find out the hard way.

So how do you actually let go or even just loosen up on expectations? First, give yourself time. There's a lot of change happening at once, and it is indeed overwhelming. It's taken a long time to become the person you are, and you will not likely break old habits overnight. For example, if you are a fastidious housekeeper—some may even call you a neat freak—the idea of going to bed with a sink full of dishes might be inconceivable. Eventually, you will have to decide if twenty more minutes of sleep—now—is more important to you than a clean kitchen.

Writing thank-you notes was a tough one for me. I would keep going until my handwriting deteriorated, and I actually remember once falling asleep while writing a note to a friend who'd sent a baby gift. But it's how I was raised. You write them, and you do it quickly. But writing a thank-you note to me is the last thing I want a new mom to be doing in her "free" time. Unless it truly makes her feel good. For the record, by my third son's premature birth, I was still writing thank-yous, but it took me months—and I never put them before visiting him in the hospital or getting sleep.

In addition to being easier on yourself, ask if there's an old way of doing things that isn't jibing with your new way of life with a newborn. Making dinner comes to mind. Countless times I'd start a meal only to have the baby need to eat or have that late afternoon period of fussiness. I would feel like a failure for not being able to make a simple meal. I'm not suggesting you "let go" of the expectation that you'll eat dinner. You need to eat and eat healthy. Just adjust your way of thinking. Cereal or PB&J for dinner is OK sometimes. So is making something easy earlier in the day—or in the week—and having it ready to pop in the oven. The Crock-Pot quickly became my greatest dinner ally.

Getting out of the house will also never be the same. It takes longer, and you will likely be late getting places sometimes.

You can beat yourself up or accept the change and look for new strategies for timing your departure better.

Talking to other moms helps. Hearing that you share the same struggles may help you adjust your way of thinking. For me, putting things on paper helps me actually see what it is I'm trying to do. Write down exactly what has to get done, and then write down what else you'd do if you could. Learn to keep your lists manageable and realistic. I realized at one point my lists were paralyzing me because they had no priorities. Painting a room and getting milk at the store were on the same notepad. My friend Michelle told me that one time she had her infant daughter in a car seat, ready to head out, when she picked up her list and took stock.

"I sat right back down and unbuckled the baby. Nothing really had to be done that moment," she said. "I realized I was keeping myself busy because I was used to working with lots of goals and deadlines. That was my biggest adjustment, adjusting my ideas on what I thought was really urgent."

## LIVING ON BABY TIME

*My Rattled Daze*

1. What did I expect life to be like when I first brought my baby home? How does reality compare to that expectation?
2. How have I adjusted my expectations of what I can accomplish in one day?
3. How do I cope with having to put some of my plans and goals on hold?

# 2

# Spin Cycle

## Taking Life One Load at a Time

It is quite normal for a new mom to feel like a hamster on a wheel. The twenty-four-hour eating and sleeping cycle of a newborn means the days run together, the days and nights certainly run together, and your pre-baby idea of what a mom-day looks like might have run away altogether. This is a short-lived yet intense period of time. By the time you finish one feeding and maybe feed yourself, it's about time to feed the baby again. Remember, this is normal and temporary.

Many women find that faithfully practicing an eat-activity-sleep pattern for their babies creates a pleasing blueprint for their days. Some found a version of this method in Tracey Hogg's *The Baby Whisperer*, while others, like me, learned it from friends and family. Having a suggested framework for your days helps you know what to expect and know what to do and when.

Here's the drill. Baby eats. Baby has awake time or play-time, no longer than fifteen minutes early on, lengthening

17

naturally as baby gets older and is more aware of his sur-roundings. Then baby is put to bed—drowsy but awake. Mak-ing sure your baby goes through each of these phases with each feeding seems to lead naturally into longer naps and that coveted through-the-night sleep for you both. Resisting the urge to feed your child until he goes to sleep is crucial in helping your baby learn to soothe himself. And it's tough for immature digestive systems to be laid down with air bubbles stuck inside, so if a baby falls asleep eating, he may not sleep long. You might diagnose your baby as a finicky sleeper, when actually he's uncomfortable from the very thing that gave him comfort—or he fell asleep before getting a full feeding. By my third son, I was a believer that usually sticking to this pattern, even waking him up gently for a few minutes if he fell asleep during a feeding, was best for creating good eating and sleeping habits. That said, being flexible and learning your own baby's patterns are essential.

I understand how easy it is to feed or hold or rock a baby to sleep. I did it for a while. The consequences seem affordable on a day-to-day basis. And it feels good. It doesn't feel good, however, when you are still doing it every nap and every night when the child is two. Investing in good sleep habits will pay huge dividends for you and your kids as they grow up.

Once the baby has a rhythm—not an unyielding schedule but a rhythm—you can take stock of your own patterns each day.

"I always thought baby days would be just sheer fun. I'd stopped working and thought I'd have all this time on my hands. To come from a job where you hand in reports and attend meetings and see things actually advance on a daily basis, mommy stuff can blow your mind in its sameness. They were fun days, but they were a little numb-ing sometimes."

Ann

"I think the part of motherhood that still makes me crazy is never seeing anything 'done,' except maybe dinner, but even that has to be done again the next day. The cycle is so mundane, the gratification so delayed. The person who weathers the first six months of mother-hood well is the person who can walk away from things with perspective, the person who can say, 'Oh well, there goes another two hours.' No one else on the planet will see the sense of urgency you do about things. Moms are just so anxious to complete things."

Lisa

Going from a work environment to being home with a baby can be a shock to the system. I was used to daily feedback. Now no one was handing out evaluations. I was used to adult interaction and decisions that would eventually reach millions of people. Now I was talking baby nonsense and was hyperfocused on one person's bowel movements.

When I was working, I planned things, created things, finished things. I didn't realize how much of a productivity junkie I was until I had a baby and couldn't get my fix.

On arrival, babies do demand, and deserve, all of you. Give it to them. And then rest. And then give them more. And then rest. You have permission to lay many of life's details aside. You are tired. And while it might give you a temporary rush of adrenalin to keep up with your old self, your new self needs time to absorb life's changes. If there is a day—or many days—that the only accomplishment you can list is taking care of the baby and maybe unloading the dishwasher, that is just fine. You will catch up on the other things soon enough. This is life with an infant.

You're thinking, *But wait, they sleep so much*! *I can do all sorts of things.* Sure, some days. But it's important not to set yourself up for frustration or failure.

Long before kids, I reported, from a Coast Guard boat, on a story about shark endangerment. I didn't know that's where I was headed that day, so my pearls and slacks made

> "All I wanted to do was sit and stare at him all day. I'm glad for that. I watched him sleep. I watched the twinkle in his eye develop. My world was consumed by that."
>
> Tristan's mom

quite a statement. Once we were out in the Gulf of Mexico, a storm blew in. The rocking and rolling of the waves threw me everywhere. I locked my knees in self-defense and tried to see through the spitting rain. I fell down more than once. And then I threw up.

The sailor who handed me a barf bag down below deck told me gently: "Your knees. You have to bend your knees so you can be ready for anything."

So it goes with daily mothering. Storms *will* arise. Rigidity can lead to a big mess. Forethought is huge. And pearls and slacks are usually not the best choice.

My sister decided to make her own birth announcements for her first child. She had them 75 percent done before he was born. We sat together one day in a sea of blue plaid scraps, happy as can be until my new nephew woke and fussed and fussed. My sister's frustration grew as he cried louder. I glued faster, he kept crying, and she kept working until we were finished. Years later we had a good laugh remembering how intense we were about something so unnecessary. Our knees were most certainly not bent.

We are a multitasking generation, and we have to be. When it's time to get three children out the door for school, you need the skills that allow you to hold cupcakes in one arm, baby in another, keys between your teeth, and the door with your foot while pleasantly urging your preschooler to leave Elmo at home and your kindergartener to flush the toilet. That was my yesterday. And I'm darn proud of it, since for a long time I could hardly feed the baby and talk on the phone at the same time. But I think sometimes we should stop layering tasks so much. My mom never talked on a cell

## Daylight

**Tips for Your Time and Spirit**

- Once your baby hits about a month old, try to begin and end your days at generally the same time. The predictability will be great for baby, and heartening for you too. Grabbing that twenty extra minutes of sleep if you can seems like a good idea, but not if it's going to make you feel behind the rest of the day.
- Shower—quickly if you have to. It's fine to do it while baby is awake—at 3 a.m. if that's what works. But shower! Having a fresh start at some point in the day makes a difference.
- Make a list to sort out the things whirling about in your head, but don't be glued to it or defeated by it. Try two sections: what must be done and what could be done. It might feel silly at first, but go ahead and write things like "Sing to my daughter" or "Tell my husband I love him" to help with prioritizing.
- Get out of the house. Maybe it's just to sweep your porch or walk to the mailbox. Sunshine and fresh air will boost your mood and remind you of life beyond your walls. If the weather is crummy, find a change of scenery in your own home. Just feeding the baby in a different room can be a pleasant change.
- Get a newspaper. Read something, however short, that has to do with current events, not about being a mom. Consider joining or starting a book club. The mental stimulation, grown-up discussion, and satisfaction of finishing something are gratifying.
- Consider ways to be productive and focused at the same time. For example, plan a day to make several dinners ahead of time and freeze them. Narrate what you're doing to your baby while he swings nearby. When a day is rocky, you'll have a good frozen meal that will help preserve a little sanity and energy at dinnertime.

phone while she drove. She didn't even drive until after she had had three children.

Children need on-their-level eye contact. That's impossible if you are too busy to bend down. The choices you make right now for you and your baby are setting a tone for your household. You can choose between a tone that's har-

21

ried and uptight or one that is flexible and peaceful. Set the right priorities during these days, and it will pay off as your children grow up.

## LIVING ON BABY TIME

*My Rattled Daze*

1. How's my rhythm? What would I like to tweak about my child's routine, and where might I seek advice?
2. What's been the toughest adjustment to motherhood for me so far?
3. How would I rate myself as a multitasker? What could help me focus more fully on my baby?

# 3

## Offbeat

### *Doing What Works for Your Family*

I still remember the look on my friend's grinning face as I sat in mommy confession with her. Today's sin: taking a shower while my new baby sat a foot away in his bouncy seat—*awake*. I was rationalizing all over the place: *He didn't seem to be too lonely; I looked out at him seven times; I was really gnarly; I usually wait until he's sleeping.*

She laughed at me and claimed my experiment was a mainstay of motherhood. "Don't you dare waste baby's nap on taking a shower!" she said. And then quite seriously she looked me in the eye and added, "Do what works for you."

Do what works for you. What anguish could be prevented if moms heard and truly believed that was okay. There is no other mom-baby combination in the universe that is you. While books give you tips, insights, and strategies, they are best used with your own mother's gut, as you create a safe, happy, and healthy place for your child to grow up. Don't think certain strategies are "wrong" until you've run them through a network of other loving, noncompetitive moms. You might already be on the right track and just don't trust yourself.

My friend Vanessa and I had our first sons six months apart. She planned out her time—even creating note cards out of *The Baby Whisperer* on creating a pattern for her new days as a mom. I remember my shock the first time I heard that Vanessa put her son down for the night at 10 p.m. She and her husband went to bed about 1 a.m. Her husband worked from home, so the whole family slept in till about 10 o'clock in the morning.

"It was different, but it worked great for us," she said. "It wasn't until talking to other people that I realized no one else was doing what we were. You learn to stand your ground

## A Day in My Life

### Putting Life in My Daze

With a newborn, it seems time is not your own. And sometimes when an unexpected pocket of peace does present itself, it can be gone before you decide what to do with it. Keep these following ideas handy to consider, and you'll probably have more and more opportunity for them as your baby grows older each week.

- **A new activity for baby**: Sing a new song, walk a different path, tell her a story about her extended family.
- **A comforting activity for me**: Call a good friend, read a new novel, take a bubble bath, record my journey in a journal.
- **An enhancing activity for my home**: Clean out a drawer, plant flowers while baby enjoys fresh air, frame or file new pictures of the baby.
- **A supportive activity for my husband**: Write a love note to reconnect, rent a movie to "share" during feeding shifts, make his favorite dessert.
- **A visionary activity for my community**: Join a local MOPS (Mothers of Preschoolers) group (www.MOPS.org), donate outgrown clothes or new baby supplies to a shelter for women and children, strike up a conversation with an elderly neighbor.

when others express their opinions. I'm sure some people thought I was weird."

I admit I was one of those people. It was hard to have a morning date to the park with Vanessa since her morning was my noon! But I admired the way her family functioned—and her confidence in her choices. She'll tell you she compared herself with other moms and wondered like the rest of us if she was doing the right thing. But when she chose a path, she didn't make excuses for it.

Sometimes the transition home with a baby feels both exciting and intimidating, like a blank canvas. There can be pressure in wanting to "draw" the perfect days, even though you are tired and just getting used to all your new responsibilities. I think it can be helpful if a new mom doesn't overscrutinize each day, but looks at her hopes and goals over time, a week perhaps. Maybe Tuesday was a day of blowout diapers and a four-feeding night, but Thursday was a trip to the mall and the chance to call your mom. Don't score each day. Rather give yourself grace; consider yourself a student learning over a very challenging school year.

Several teacher friends shared with me how they brought their training to bear and started writing a "lesson plan" for their days as new moms. It wasn't a strict, teach-your-newborn-his-colors lesson plan, but more of a personal strategy for getting through the day and getting a few things done. Even a list maker like me hadn't thought of trying to put into words the overall mission for my days—especially with the busyness of a new baby. If I had done this, it might have cleared the fog a little.

"It held me accountable when I felt like no one was holding me accountable," one teacher friend, Erika, told me.

"All the books said you should get up before your child to get that head start. I was never good at that, but I still needed a way to get centered each day. I would get up and feed the baby and put her back in her crib with the mobile on. I got ready pretty quickly, but as I got ready, I lit a candle each day.

"I would say, 'God, give me the strength to do what you want me to do today.' It just gave me a little inner peace, a quiet ahhh moment. I thought if *I* needed that to get started, my daughter did too. So we both got that time. My kids still get that time as I get ready. The candle was just a great trick for me."

You'll likely discover plenty of tricks in the coming years, such as peaceful grocery shopping at 10 p.m., when your husband is home to babysit; throwing pureed vegetables into brownies for the nutritional value; or hiding dryer sheets under your seat to get rid of that smell in your car. Enjoy the journey of discovery, and remember, finding your family's groove takes a while. What works with one baby might not work with the next. What works one *week* might not work the next. My hope is that you are able, in the weary excitement of this precious time, to see that while you don't control your time as you used to, you do have options and the freedom to try out those options.

## LIVING ON BABY TIME

### My Rattled Daze

1. What works for me? Do I like a scheduled day or an unscheduled day?
2. What's one thing I can do daily to help me feel some sort of routine exists in my life right now?
3. How have I tailored my routine to my family's needs?

# 4

## Staying Flexible

### *What Rattles Your Rhythm*

Perhaps it is no accident that during the days I was writing this chapter, my two-and-a-half-year-old threw up on me. Two days later I walked away from the computer to find my five-and-a-half-year-old tossing his cookies too. There was a time that this would have thrown my entire week into a tizzy of doctor calls and hourly husband updates and major anxiety. Barfing babies scared me.

Over time I've become much less tightly wound about things I can't control. It can be a beautiful benefit of motherhood, this mellowing out, especially since the days *without* craziness or crisis can sometimes feel like the abnormal ones. At this moment I have a jumbo bottle of window cleaner under my sink, with a table knife lodged in it. I'm pretty sure I know which kid did it and when—can't imagine why—but I've decided not to make it a big deal. After spending five minutes a day trying to get the knife out, ensuring my fingers would smell like ammonia for a month, I just had to laugh and move on. There it sits under the sink.

A few weeks ago my toddler son snuck in the kitchen and tried earnestly to make hot chocolate all by himself. I really battle with the nonstop goo in my house these days and how it makes me feel unkempt as a woman and as a housekeeper. The gritty brown sludge I saw *coating* him and my kitchen could have sent me over the edge. Instead it sent me to the camera to record a moment in time—in his time—that was actually quite beautiful.

I can imagine your eyes rolling. But trust me, it took a while for this control freak to get to this place. And I'm not always there.

Poet Maya Angelou says you can tell a lot about a person by how he or she handles lost luggage, a rainy day, and tangled Christmas tree lights. Curse words and foot stomping come to mind? Those won't help you much as a mom. Good baggage tags, an umbrella kept where you need it, and a sense of humor will get you much farther—in a word, *preparation*. Here are some things known to throw moms into a frenzy, and some ideas on persevering through them.

## Doctor Visits and Immunizations

A visit to the pediatrician was often a high point in my weeks as a new mom. Not only did it force me out, but I found out how much weight my baby had gained. Each new ounce felt like a validation of all I was giving and going through at home. But I struggled with finding the right time for each visit. When you are feeding a baby around the clock, it's pretty hard to time an appointment so it doesn't coincide with a feeding during the trip to or from or actually in the doctor's office. Don't try too hard. Doctors see plenty of fussy babies and moms who nurse while they wait.

Just the stimulation of the visit can make baby cry, and immunizations can make you both want to cry. Seeing your baby poked by a needle may be harder on you than on the baby. When doctors' appointments came in the morning, I always planned to do something for myself—at home—in the afternoon. The shots seemed to bring on a deep afternoon nap for the baby, which I was willing to let go a little longer knowing what he'd been through.

Shots can also result in fussiness and a low-grade fever in the days to come, so I tried not to plan outings during those days—and I always had infant Tylenol on hand.

If doctor's appointments seem challenging to you, time them near your husband's lunch hour so he can go along, or ask Grandma to accompany you for support. Many years after my first baby's doctor's visits, I still write down the issues or questions I want to cover with the doctor. I simply can't remember them all on my own while dealing with kids in an exam room.

## Growth Spurts

Growth spurts are otherwise known as confidence thieves. Baby gets fussy, seems to eat nonstop, or starts waking at night just when you thought the stretches of sleep were getting longer. You wonder about your milk production. You question your choice of formula. Your husband questions you. Your frustration simmers. You thought you had this down.

*Stay the course!* Growth spurts can happen at any time, but watch for them at about seven to ten days old, two to three weeks, four to six weeks, three months, four months, six months, and nine months old. They can last a couple of days or up to a week.

Respond to your baby's signals. If he's hungry, feed him. Nursing moms will see their milk production catch up with baby's demands in a day or so. Keep drinking lots of water. For formula babies, the American Academy of Pediatrics recommends that babies take in about two and one-half ounces of formula a day for every pound of body weight. Do your math and make sure you are keeping pace. Also consider that if your baby is sleeping longer at night, he may need more milk during the day. If your child is older than four months, he may be showing signs of being ready for cereal. Discuss this with your doctor.

How do you know that this burst of certainty-busting was really growth? Look for your child to sleep a little harder or longer for a couple of days and for your breasts and baby's diapers to feel fuller. Watch for this pattern to repeat itself and don't get discouraged. Your intuition is being honed with each growth spurt you identify. One day you'll see the signs clearly in your growing toddler.

## Illness

There is nothing harder than trying to parent when you long to jump in bed and wallow in the misery of a cold. Your head is pounding, your eyes are watering, and your throat is scratchy. Anyone else would pick up the phone and take a sick day. Moms rarely get one.

It's just as draining emotionally as physically to be a sick mom. You experience an odd combination of feeling trapped, guilty, and resentful. Those feelings, while valid, aren't going to help you get better. If you are in need of help, you must find it. Ask your husband to stay home. If you don't tell him, he doesn't know how clogged your head is or how bad that tooth hurts.

If you do have to muddle through on your own, be careful about the medicine you take for relief, especially making sure it's safe if you are nursing. You don't want a drug making you too fuzzy to function. Let go of the housework for a while, and know that it's okay to curl up with a blanket on the floor as your baby plays in a safe, contained area.

Don't spread germs by going to your playgroups or other commitments. Calling in reinforcements to help you is tricky since you don't want to expose anyone else to your illness. But if your baby is well, consider asking a friend to take her for a walk. Other moms would probably be happy to get you a few groceries, even if they choose to leave them on your porch. Wouldn't you do the same? Creating that go-to network will never happen if someone doesn't make the first move. Having it in place is a beautiful thing.

My friend Sara is among those tough-as-nails women who are sick nearly their entire pregnancies. Trying to parent a child, while growing a child, while throwing up every day, gave her a new perspective on trying to do it all. "Your children will not remember that you pawned them off for a few days," she says. "You cannot be afraid to take the help when you need it. That's exactly what you'd tell a friend, so you have to listen to yourself."

Preventing illness takes on new meaning when your job is 24-7. Stay healthy by getting all the sleep you can and taking a multivitamin. And here's a plug for hand washing: there is no better way to keep your kids or yourself from getting sick. It's not the soap you use; it's how long you wash. Twenty seconds at the sink can help keep colds as well as serious respiratory illnesses and diarrhea at bay.

## Sleep Struggles

Perhaps nothing requires more patience and flexibility from a mom than her child's sleep habits. Volumes have been written on how to cultivate healthy nap and bedtime practices, and there is much sound advice to be had. I'd be remiss if I didn't mention the family-changing potential of books like *The Baby Whisperer*; *Sleep Solutions for Your*

*Baby, Toddler, and Preschooler*; and *Healthy Sleep Habits, Happy Child*. Thank goodness these resources exist. Use them; highlight them; put them to the test. However, *your* approach to sleep is a chapter only *you* can write. It needs to include humor, flexibility, realistic expectations, and the acknowledgment that every child is different and no phase is forever.

I have a few thoughts on riding out the waves of sleep inconsistencies. Make sure you are parenting a person, not a schedule. As this book began, I recounted how I fought against my son's sleep instead of rolling with it. Someone reminded me along the way that we adults don't just fall asleep with the flick of a switch at someone else's discretion. Far from it. Our minds spin, our stomachs rumble, or the noises of the night keep us from settling down. Remembering this helped—and still helps—when I get frustrated with a non-napper or early riser. It also helps me to know that sleep isn't something to fool around with. It's a sound place to invest your parental energy and creativity. Being consistent—again not rigid—with naps and bedtimes produces a good sleeper, which in turn means a healthier child who learns better and is generally in a better mood.

It still amazes me that overtired children fight sleep. It goes against conventional wisdom, doesn't it? *I'll keep him up longer so he'll plunge into a three-hour nap. I'll let him stay up Friday night so he'll sleep in Saturday morning.* It doesn't work that way. If you miss a baby or child's drowsy window and he gets too tired, falling asleep could involve some serious fussing, and you may have unwittingly set the stage for a shorter nap.

I had a few other sleep "awakenings" too. My oldest stopped settling well into an afternoon nap at about six months old. I struggled and struggled and finally it dawned on me—he needed lunch. Sound obvious? I was a first-time mom, a first-time feeder of jar foods. I'd started with breakfast and then added dinner, as my pediatrician suggested. I just never thought much about lunch. But extra calories made an instant difference. When he got older, a similar wakefulness happened again at naptime. I started taking him out, playing a little while, and then trying again. Seems he wasn't tired anymore at the naptime I'd established. So I had to go with his flow—his own drowsy times. A half-hour change solved the problem. It was a great lesson for me.

Remember to go with your baby's flow when one day it comes time for her to drop a nap. It will rearrange your schedule, but your schedule is not effective unless it suits your child. This makes sense, and though it's good to read about the proper care of baby, often we must just go with our common sense.

## How Much Sleep Do They Need?

This guide is a compilation of what pediatricians and parenting experts advise for sleep. Don't fret if your child is off a bit, but straying too far from these sleep amounts could create a foundation for fussiness and growth challenges. Consult your pediatrician if your child's wakefulness is a concern.

| Age | Number of Naps | Total Sleep Hours |
| --- | --- | --- |
| 1 week | through the day | 16.5 |
| 1 month | 3 | 15.5 |
| 3 months | 3 | 15 |
| 6 months | 2 | 14.25 |
| 9 months | 2 | 14 |
| 12 months | 2 | 13.75 |
| 18 months | 1 | 13.5 |
| 2 years | 1 | 13 |
| 3 years | 1 | 12 |
| 4 years | 0 | 11–12 |
| 5 years | 0 | 11 |
| 10 years | 0 | 9.75 |
| adolescent | 0 | 9.25* |

*they usually get about 7.5 hours due to biological rhythms and early school start times

## Teething

It's a joke in our house with any low-grade fever or crankiness to blame it on teething. I think my husband even asked *me* once: "New teeth coming in?" Whether or not that's the source of the angst, it's nice to blame it on something. Teething usually begins between four and nine months, with at least a first tooth forming a gum bump and then popping through by the time baby turns one. That said, I've seen a child get that first chomper at four months, and another pop one at thirteen and a half months. First to show up is usually the bottom front pair of incisors, but two of my sons got their top ones first—very beaveresque!

Children handle teething differently. My nephew wore drool-drenched clothes for several months. I hardly saw spit when my boys were teething. In time the range of teething symptoms gets easier to spot and pull together in your mind as you assess what's going on with your baby. Those symptoms include irritability, drooling, disturbed sleep, an extra-saliva cough without a cold or flu, and gnawing on anything they can hold. Eating irregularities—like pursing lips to keep the spoon out—can also point to a mouth in pain.

Not all doctors agree that diarrhea and a low-grade fever are linked to teething, but I'd swear they are. When those symptoms last more than a couple days you should consult your pediatrician. When you consider all that kids are putting in their mouths, as well as the is-there-a-tooth-in-there checks you may be doing, the fever could be a sign of illness. It's imperative to keep yours and baby's hands clean to keep germs from adding illness to teething woes.

If your child is having a rough teething day, consider tanking your plans for the day. It's not convenient, but when's the last time *you* tried to put on a smile and have a normal day with a toothache? Teething rings can be helpful, although that was the one thing my kids *wouldn't* chew on. The numbing gels just annoyed them. Ibuprofen or acetaminophen, given with a doctor's approval, was the only thing that gave my kids relief.

## Introducing a Bottle

If you ask a number of nursing moms if, when, and how you should introduce a bottle, you'll get no consensus. Some women wait just a few weeks after birth to introduce a bottle, but their babies refuse to take it. Others wait a few months, and their kids seem not to have any confusion about going back and forth. If you want baby and bottle to be friends, and they're not, it can be very troubling.

On the rare occasions we would leave our oldest son, Zach, with a babysitter for an evening, we'd come home to find he had taken perhaps an ounce from a bottle. I'd crumple in guilt. Our youngest, A.J., went happily between a bottle and me until pneumonia put him in the hospital. Then I was all too happy to nurse him exclusively because it seemed to be the one thing I could do to comfort him. He never took a bottle again. I was disappointed and kept trying, but there wasn't any guilt this time because I realized that I could try a cup at any time and he wasn't going to starve. Dozens of women I know have experienced the joy of nursing with the baggage of not ever being able to leave baby and a bottle behind successfully. Try giving your baby a cup, and try not to worry. When baby begins eating solids, his tummy will fill up, and you can spend time away from him knowing he will be satisfied. If you are at ease about this, your husband or caregiver will be too. Don't use your baby's refusal to take a bottle as an excuse not to take breaks from home and baby. Nursing loses much of its benefit if you get resentful.

## Trusting Your Instincts

Sometimes newer moms feel inferior to those with more children and more experience, and they're tempted to ditch their own instincts. I was especially prone to this on trips and around relatives. For example, say you are at the park with some new friends. You feel your child is nearing naptime, but so far she's doing well, and you don't want to seem like a sleep Nazi, so you stick around. The other mothers don't seem concerned about naptime and *they must know what they are doing, right*? Twenty minutes later, your baby erupts into wails of overstimulation, and your park departure and drive home are miserable.

Enough uncontrollable things rattle your rhythm as a mom without you doing it to yourself, just because you want to fit

## Picture This

The adrenalin was pumping.

Not only had I been a mom for just thirteen days, but I was with my parents—first-time, adoring grandparents—and we were on a mission to get Zach's first picture. Sort of the Bermuda Triangle of common sense.

We arrived at Kiddie Kandids and put our names on a list. I had enough experience in my thirteen days to know I needed to feed Zach while I could. My dad wandered through babyland, and Mom accompanied me to the lounge. Zach nursed as we heard muffled names being called over the store's intercom.

I started to change the baby when my dad banged on the door, telling us it was our turn. At that very moment, Zach's exposed penis shot pee through the air with such force that it showered both his head and the wall behind him. The outfit was spared, barely.

We made it to the cameras, at which point I brought out the little hat that went with the outfit that was drowning him, though the tag told me it should fit. The hat was too big too, but I was so insistent he wear it, that we paper clipped it together in the back.

Well, we survived and got some great pictures to boot. My sweet boy was so exhausted that he conked out on the living room couch. My dog curled up next to him in virtually the same position for her own nap. Now that was a good picture.

I've been through the picture-taking ordeal many times since—minus the projectile pee. Often I get anxious and start to sweat, but the experience is always a reminder of our limits as moms.

Here are some tips for enjoying the experience.

• If your photographer can't handle the rhythms of children with patience and compassion, find another one.

in or put on a good face. You are the only one who is mom to your child. No one else will protect his naps, anticipate his meals, or care about the condition of his rear end quite like you. When you embrace this fact, you become not just your child's biological beginning but his advocate.

On the flip side is the mom who can't admit she's learning and is so staunch in her ideas and paralyzed by her sched-

- Try for the morning's first appointment or walk-in opportunity.
- Take a helper. Having another set of hands is great, especially when multiple kids are involved in the photo.
- Beware of feeding your child seconds before you manhandle her, if you want clothes to stay clean. Get her to produce a good burp.
- Forget overalls. While darling on a hanger, they bunch up and gap in weird places on children who can't stand.
- Your attitude is everything, and children sense your unease. Have fun with it. You don't want a picture that screams "My mom made me do this."
- Chop the props. A rocker or wagon is nice, but be wary of using so many add-ins that your child is lost in the shuffle. What seems like a good idea in the studio can later appear to be busy, hokey pictures. You can't go wrong with a sweet face—smiling or not—and a white background.
- Check your expectations at the door. My first attempt at having two kids photographed together resulted in a picture of Zach holding a sleeping newborn Luke. He simply couldn't stay awake. Oh well, it was real life.
- If you are photographing just one of your children and your other children are young, make sure they have something to do during the process or something to look forward to when it's over. With the photographer's permission, enlist their help in keeping the subject entertained and smiling. Sometimes they're best at it!
- Be willing to call it a day if your child is howling and you feel yourself starting to lose your patience. No picture is worth stressing out either of you.
- Consider waiting to order photos. Choose to come back rather than make a selection with a crying infant needing you. Many women have wished they had stepped back before ordering more pictures than they needed or choosing one that later didn't seem to capture the child they know.

ule that she drives others away. Make no mistake, we are all learning, all the time.

A word on the mom with three kids or more, the one you see deftly steering a double stroller and maybe holding hands with another child. You wonder, *How in the world would I do three when I can barely do one?* Please don't get ahead of yourself. Yes, one seems easy by comparison when you have two or three or four children. But there's not a mom in the world who hasn't felt her hands completely full with her first child. She is lying if she says otherwise, or she has a highly selective memory.

## LIVING ON BABY TIME

*My Rattled Daze*

1. What rattles me the most? How could I change my reaction to that?
2. How can I listen to the advice of other moms without thinking I have to follow their pattern completely? What would help me sift through it all and decide what is right for my baby and me?
3. How can I involve my husband in decisions I must make about baby's sleep, seeking a doctor's advice, and other choices I must make daily?

# 5

## Tears and Fears

### *Coping with Crying*

Sometimes the unique direction our days take is not of our choosing. Colic throws many families for a loop. This phenomenon of hours-long crying usually hits your baby suddenly and in the evening. The National Institutes of Health says about 20 percent of babies cry enough to meet the definition of colic, which begins most often when baby is three weeks old and usually lifts by twelve weeks.

Like many moms whose babies have colic, my friend Liz's "lesson plan" for her day was simply survival. She'd put on headphones each night and hold a screaming infant, something she had to do for both her children.

"Someone gave me the analogy of thinking what it would be like to go to a foreign country where you didn't speak the language and couldn't communicate with a soul. That's your miserable baby," Liz said. "It helped me, seeing it like that. It allowed me not to get angry at my kids but to just feel sad for them. I felt like I was the only one dealing with it, and it felt like an eternity."

Motherhood tests us all, but colic is like a twelve-week bar exam—beyond intense. The parent of a colicky baby knows a different depth of uncertainty and vulnerability.

Hang in there. Your child needs you.

The more your baby cries, the more you want to be the one to soothe, the one to provide the breakthrough. Please, take a break. Take a walk. Even just an hour away can refuel you. Your baby needs *you*, not the hollow-eyed, crazy lady you will become if you don't step away once in a while. Friends and neighbors want to help. Let them. Share your struggles verbally too. It's normal to feel angry or down. Be willing to vent.

When your child cries incessantly—colic or not—it is normal to have moments where you feel like you are losing control of your own emotions. This was especially true for me when I was alone with my first child. I just kept hanging on to him and hoping it would stop. No one ever told me it was okay to lay down a shrieking baby and move away to collect myself. What a simple and potentially life-saving piece of insight!

Now, years later, I don't know many moms who haven't at some point put their crying child down in a crib, closed the door, and then sat outside the door and cried. Whether he's four months or four years, it's very difficult to hear your child's anguish. It does get easier when you realize his pain—getting a new tooth, scraping a knee, earning a time-out—is not your fault. But when the cries are from a helpless baby, and especially your first, I know what I'm suggesting sounds harsh. But if your arms aren't helping, give them a rest. Put

"She would start crying at 5 p.m. and go till about 9:30. Of course Brian was home then, so that was all he saw of her. You feel like you have to fix it, to do the right thing. The noise of your baby's cry affects you like nothing else. You feel so helpless. But accepting that, that you are sort of helpless, was a huge turning point in my getting through it."

Liz

"I spent way too much time looking online for answers, doubting my own milk supply and researching alternatives. Finally I had to quit driving myself mad with all the information out there and just accept that it was something he was just going to have to go through and the best I could do was love him through it. I replayed an internal tape in my head telling myself that this was temporary and eventually it would only be a distant memory."

Noell

the baby in his crib. Splash water on your face, breathe deeply, and pull yourself together. If you need to, call for help.

Sadly, there's a reason the National Center on Shaken Baby Syndrome exists. When a frustrated caregiver loses control with an inconsolable baby, it takes as little as *five seconds* of shaking to alter that fragile life forever. When you shake a baby, her brain can actually bounce around in her skull. The resulting trauma can mean brain damage, blindness, lifelong disability, or—as in 25 percent of babies with shaken baby syndrome—death.

Think you are too educated or too in control for such an emotional reaction to a crying baby? I hope you never have that theory tested, but it's safer to have a plan of action when you reach your limit. Discuss these realities with your husband and whoever else cares for your child. Tell them what happens when a baby is shaken. Tell them it's fine to call you for help.

Remember that your child's crying is not a reflection of your mommying—your caring attitude is.

## Ideas for Comforting Baby

- Feed your baby. If you think your baby may be hungry, try a feeding. Hold your baby as upright as possible, and burp your baby often. Sometimes more frequent—but smaller—feedings are helpful. If you're breast-feeding, it may help to empty one breast completely before switching sides. This will give your baby more hindmilk, which is richer and potentially more satisfying than the foremilk present at the beginning of a feeding. Foremilk is the milk, typically lower in fat, available at the beginning of a feeding; hindmilk is milk at the end of a feeding which has a higher fat content than the foremilk. You can even see the darker color and thicker consistency to the milk that is produced at the end of a session, as opposed to the beginning.
- Offer a pacifier. For many babies, sucking is a soothing activity. Even if you're breast-feeding, it's okay to offer a pacifier to help your baby calm down.
- Hold your baby. Cuddling helps some babies. Some will quiet when they're held closely and swaddled in a lightweight blanket. To give your arms a break, try a baby sling, backpack, or other type of baby carrier. Don't worry about spoiling your baby by holding her too much. Spoiled children have learned to use behavior to get what they want. Your newborn is too young to purposefully manipulate you.
- Keep your baby in motion. Gently rock your baby in your arms or in an infant swing. Lay your baby, tummy down, on your knees and then sway your knees slowly. Take a walk with your baby, or buckle your baby in the car seat for a drive. Use a vibrating infant seat or vibrating crib.
- Sing to your baby. A soft tune might soothe him. And even if lullabies don't stop your baby from crying, they can keep you calm and help pass the time while you're waiting for him to settle down. Playing recorded music may help too.
- Turn up the background noise. Some babies cry less when they hear steady background noise. When holding or rocking your baby, try making a continuous "shhhhh" sound. Turn on a kitchen or bathroom exhaust fan, or play a tape or CD of environmental sounds, such as ocean waves, a waterfall, or gentle rain. Sometimes the tick of a clock or metronome does the trick.
- Use gentle heat or touch. Give your baby a warm bath. Softly massage her, especially around the tummy.
- Look for hidden aggravation. Check for diaper rash. Check for those little plastic strands that connect tags to new clothes. Check your calendar to see if teething could be a factor.

- Give your baby some private time. If nothing else seems to work, a brief time-out might help. Put your baby in his crib for five to ten minutes.
- Consider dietary changes. If you breast-feed, see if eliminating certain foods from your own diet—such as dairy products, citrus fruits, spicy foods, or drinks containing caffeine—has any effect on your baby's crying. If you use a bottle, a new type of bottle or nipple might help.
- Mix it up. Experiment to discover what works best for your baby, even if it changes from day to day.

## LIVING ON BABY TIME

### My Rattled Daze

1. When my baby cries and I can't comfort her, what do I do?
2. Do I believe it's okay to give myself a time-out and put my baby in a safe place for five to ten minutes when he is crying inconsolably?
3. How is my baby sleeping? Where could I find extra support and good ideas to establish my baby's good sleep habits?

# 6

## Just One More Thing

*Leaving the House*

Finding your rhythm at home is challenging enough. Thinking about taking your show on the road can be downright scary. It's a roller coaster you know you need to force yourself to ride. We start looking forward to the wind in our hair and hope to be survivors at the end, but we're pretty darn nervous about what can happen in the middle.

In leaving the house with a baby, one of the most important skills of mothering comes into play: *thinking ahead*. Every day millions of moms do mental gymnastics as they try to anticipate their baby's needs—and it doesn't stop as the child grows. When will she be hungry enough to eat but not so hungry she loses it? What's the best diversion while we wait in line to get the car inspected? How long can we stay at the zoo so she naps at home, not in the car? How can I stuff that piece of gum in my mouth without having to explain why we can't all have one? How long do I realistically have to try on a new pair of jeans with two children in a dressing room the size of a phone booth?

Make no mistake, this anticipating is a skill acquired over time. Don't berate yourself for the goofs you will inevitably make, the moments you'll try to gracefully back out of a situation gone awry. But if you can look at "thinking ahead" as something to learn, like good swaddling or how to spoon-feed a baby without sliming yourself, I think you'll be rewarded. Don't let the anticipation of the what-ifs scare you into staying put. Let them boost your confidence. You need to know how to go and where to go. Notice that "whether to go" is not an option. You need to get out.

That was me one morning. I had made a list of things I needed but could have lived without. If I'd had the courage to write on the list "be around grown-ups," it would have been on the top line. So on this day getting dog food and toothpaste was a great excuse to visit Target.

I had learned not to push my two-month-old's feeding schedule if at all possible, so we stopped in the back of the café area to nurse before shopping. As I sat there happy as can be—feeling composed, feeding this awesome creature, enjoying being out—he pooped. And I mean pooped. The sound was so long and so liquid and gathered so much attention that I started to laugh, until I realized it had exploded out of his diaper, soaked through his onesie, and gotten all over me.

I didn't have extra clothes and really didn't have the stomach to depoop my baby in a public sink. So we were done. I was more amazed than angry at how my morning plans had been derailed. How a person so little could have such a big impact on my time! It was a lesson I learned again and again—that and to always take a fresh baby outfit anywhere you go.

There's a joke among experienced mothers that you can always tell a new mom by how bulging her diaper bag is. In the beginning, you take everything. If that makes you feel more comfortable getting out, then do it. You are not being

> "I went to Babies R Us more than I needed to simply because there were people like me there. I remember my first trip to the mall. I was so proud. I fed her. I changed her. And then she projectile vomited—all the way from the car seat in the stroller to a rack of Liz Claiborne clothes. Being the responsible mother I was, I ran."
>
> Liz

mocked. We've all been there. Keep in mind that the more you take, the more you have to lose, literally. Shoes for a baby who can't yet roll over, the extra hat, the extra blanket, the six toys "just in case." You increase your odds of losing the diaper bag itself if it's so big you have to continually set it down. If you are running a quick errand, consider just putting a diaper and wipes in your purse and leaving the bag in the car.

I went through three diaper bags before I settled on a rather plain black diaper backpack that has been just awesome. My husband is quite comfortable carrying it, it gives me free arms in an airport, and I'm sure it will still be used when diapers aren't.

Take Ziplocs or plastic grocery bags in whatever diaper bag you use. They are priceless for getting soggy or poopy clothes home or containing a stinky diaper when there's no trash can in sight.

My friend Erika calls her get-ready-to-go area her "launch pad." It consists of a couple rows of hooks at kid-friendly heights, each for a bag prepacked for a given activity. Baby's bag, ballet practice bag, the library bag, and so on. There are hooks designated for coats too. Bags have a home, and they get repacked not in the flurry of an impending departure, but when they are put back on the hook each day.

I hang one of those see-through plastic shoe holders behind my mudroom door, but not for shoes. Everything from sun-screen to mittens to downstairs toothbrushes lives in there to help in getting away from the house without seventeen trips upstairs. Keep diapers on every level of your home and in hiding places in your car too. In the car, a small, see-through plastic tub for each of your children can help you be prepared with toys, snacks, an extra pacifier, emergency formula, a backup T-shirt, and whatever else the child may need.

Establishing smart habits and your out-and-about rhythm with baby number one will serve you well as your family grows.

My kids used to think it was a game, seeing how many times mommy would run back inside the house for something while everyone was strapped in and ready for takeoff. Once when my parents were in town, we decided to go to the zoo. The car was loaded up with kids, grandparents, and supplies. About the sixth time I got out of the car to get something else, I thought Dad was going to lose it, and my kids no longer found it humorous. It is what it is. I call it colander brain. Inevitably, like slippery strands of spaghetti in a colander, one or two of my thoughts slide out of my brain. And so I go back inside to retrieve that one more thing. I'm getting better, but I've just accepted that no matter how many lists I make, this is the way I am.

For many years I was also known for being late. I used the kids as an excuse, even when they weren't the holdup. I'd joke that I was three weeks late coming out of the womb and had been behind ever since. There's a difference in being on kid time and just being late all the time. It took kindergarten to change my ways. I truly struggled with getting three kids out the door to arrive within the prescribed ten-minute window. But knowing it reflected on my son, I made it work. Not only did I learn to give myself the appropriate amount of time,

"At the beginning of parenting, not being efficient and quick was a huge adjustment for me, one of the toughest. Now that I'm used to toddler time, it'll be hard to see petty things as time critical when I go back to work full-time."

Angela

"In the workplace you get so much attention as a woman who is pregnant with her first baby. And then you are forgotten, and you forget there's a world beyond the walls of your home. So you take your two-week survival diaper bag and you go to the mall. I spent so much time in the Nordstrom lounge. I think William grew up there. I just wanted to be around other women. I didn't know them, but we were interested in each other. We were all there because we needed to get out of the house. That lounge saved my life. I was hungry for company."

Susan

but I used the time more and more effectively. It mattered, and so I made it happen.

Back in the days of walking the mall with a baby, being on time was the last thing on my mind, even if I was meeting a friend.

Ah, the mall! Where I live, the stroller rodeo starts early under the skylights and around the huge fireplaces of a real shopping beauty. It's a great place to practice getting out with baby. The Nordstrom department store lounge is more like a living room than a ladies' room. Spending time there is a rite of passage for new moms. Women gather to change and nurse babies, bond for three minutes at a time with total strangers, and feel purposeful, as though they are part of a movement. (And I don't mean bowel.)

There's probably a place of similar connection in your area. If you aren't sure, start asking. Maybe it has nothing to do with shopping—but that's highly unlikely. The only downside to a mall is the temptation to spend money. But dozens of women have told me that, besides buying Starbucks coffee or maybe lunch at the food court, they didn't have to spend money to feel great being there, and they became great sale hounds to boot.

Recently a friend told me she thought the mall appealed to moms because it's a place of guaranteed order when your life is anything but. It's bright and cheery, and other people pick

## When Women Cocoon

Some women are more comfortable staying at home with a new baby. Maybe constant spitting or colicky crying make leaving the house seem too overwhelming. Perhaps nursing in public is too daunting, or you're self-conscious about how you look. One friend told me of staying in because her son hadn't pooped for several days, and she just didn't want to be out when he finally did!

Each mom must proceed at her own pace. And certainly there are days when staying home in your pajamas is highly appealing and downright nurturing. However, if constant tears or feelings of sadness or regret are keeping you inside, consider that you might be experiencing postpartum depression.

The signs include restlessness or irritability; feeling sad, hopeless, and overwhelmed; crying a lot; having no energy or motivation; eating too little or too much; sleeping too little or too much; trouble focusing, remembering, or making decisions; feeling worthless and guilty; a loss of interest or pleasure in activities; withdrawal from friends and family; thoughts of hurting the baby; or a lack of interest in the baby.

If you are experiencing symptoms—which are the result of hormonal shifts and the stresses in your life—talk to your doctor. Postpartum depression is quite treatable with medicine or therapy. It's helpful not to spend a lot of time alone. Open the blinds and let sunlight in. Get dressed and leave the house. Run an errand or take a short walk. Share, share, share.

Millions of women have experienced this fog. It *will* lift.

For more information on postpartum depression, check out Part 2, *Your Body after Baby*.

up after you. I also think it's a connection to who we used to be—up on fashion, perhaps with our own income to spend, and surely with a different goal to our wandering. You may not fit as well into other places you used to frequent before baby.

Consider the movies. On the one hand, a sleepy newborn might nurse and nuzzle just fine while you escape into a film. On the other hand, people often go to the movies as a grown-up activity, and a crying infant isn't welcome. Once while out of town, we took our five-month-old to a late movie. He did sleep, eventually, but what I remember is our nervousness as new parents. I've completely forgotten the film.

If you go to a movie and can tolerate some disapproving stares from people expecting the worst when they see you bringing a baby, remember a few things. Consider a late weeknight show when there are lighter crowds. Bring soothing objects for the baby, like a pacifier or a blankie. Time your movie so baby will eat about fifteen minutes into the show. Use lots of hand sanitizer to prevent spreading germs.

Going out to dinner with a baby might seem like a cakewalk after you try a movie! Again, timing is everything. Avoid places with long waits and too much stimulation (blaring music and TVs in every corner) and smoke. Expect to switch

## How Do I Love You?

### Let Me Count the Places . . .

Need some good ideas for getting out with baby?

- Meet your husband for lunch.
- Find a MOPS group (MOPS.org) for fellowship with other moms. Child care is provided!
- Try the library. Taking your baby to story time is not ridiculous. It introduces her to a social setting, and it's never too early to read to a child. You can pick up some mental stimulation in the grown-up section at the same time. The same goes for a bookstore. Pick one with a coffee bar!
- Go for a drive to a new place with the windows down and your favorite music up.
- Peruse craft shows, farmers markets, and museums.
- Walk the mall with some other moms.
- When your baby is about six months old, look for swim classes, sign language classes, or mom-and-me exercise classes at the local recreation center.
- Sit in your yard on a blanket with your baby or visit the park—yes, even with a newborn. Enjoy the serendipity of your day—and the temporary immobility of your child. Take the camera and get some sunlit photographs. These days may seem long, but the years fly by.

off with your dinner partner if baby is awake and needs to be held. To this day it still seems that my husband and I are always eating in shifts—together but in shifts.

The older your baby gets, the more challenging all outings will be as he gets more vocal, more mobile, and more demanding. Get out there with your newborn and sow the seeds of self-confidence. Remember that wherever you go, you can always leave. It's not what happens to you, it's how you react to it. You don't get pass or fail marks for outings, just wisdom.

## LIVING ON BABY TIME

*My Rattled Daze*

1. What's been my most successful outing? What made it feel that way?
2. What's something I've learned about leaving the house that I'll definitely share with another new mom?
3. What new outing will I try with my newborn? Will I ask someone to go with me or will it just be the baby and me?

# 7

## Two Jobs to Do

### *Rhythms of a Working Mom*

Kim had just had her first daughter, but back in the office she had no choice but to hit the ground running. A new product was being launched, and she had to fill her seat in the conference room. There wasn't even time to set up her desk.

Sitting in the daylong meeting, her body and the clock told her it was time to pump. "I started to get up," she said. "I was told, 'It is not appropriate for you to leave right now.' So I couldn't get up. I was leaking. I can still remember what I was wearing it was such a vivid moment. Life had changed. I was soaking. This was not how I had envisioned the 'having it all' working mom scenario.

"What I longed for more than anything was some simple empathy, rather than continual stare downs as I excused myself from one meeting after another."

Finding your rhythm as a new mom is tough enough. Returning to work adds many new out-of-tune notes to the song your life is trying to sing. All new moms are trying to

"I am a better mom in the long run for my kids when I get away and work. I would be a horrible mommy if I were home all the time without a work identity. I spent fourteen years as a career woman, eight with Universal Studios. It was who I was, and so it was pretty tough to give that up for a while. I love being a mom, but it wasn't my dream from the time I was ten."

Elizabeth

establish themselves in an overwhelming role. All new moms are making sacrifices. All new moms have a stew of fluctuating hormones and emotions that can slow them down. All new moms have to figure out a way to leave the house with a little person in tow.

For a working mom, all of these challenges must be done in front of co-workers, bosses, and caregivers, not to mention others who judge her decision and expect her former self to show up for work. It's tough, but with organization and a clear sense of your motives, it's doable.

Be honest about the reasons you are staying home or going back to work. Write down the pros and cons and then check them periodically. As you get to know your baby, you will also become better acquainted with the emotional and financial realities of your growing family. Today's decisions might change tomorrow. Go to work but know why you are going. Stay home but be clear on what you are trying to accomplish.

"I write down my motives, my goals. I've tacked them on my bathroom wall and left them in the car. They have to be readily available because I get swayed every single day," my friend Katie relates. "My daughter cut her chin recently, and it was the longest twenty-five-minute ride of my life from work to be with her. I wanted to be the one with the Band-aid. I beat them to the hospital. And there I was again, having to make sure I'm clear on why I'm doing what I'm doing."

In my case, I spent six years trying to have children. In the beginning I assumed day care—a crisp, cute one I had in mind—

## Decisions, Decisions

Child Care Aware is a national toll-free information line and website for families making child care decisions. There's a great decision-making tool on the website that allows families to organize their thoughts, consider the impact of their decisions, and review the options for finding child care in their area. It's an operation of the National Association of Child Care Resource and Referral Agencies. Check out www.childcareaware.org or call 1-800-424-2246.

would become a part of my life. The more I wanted children, the more I was in touch with what I wanted to give, not just what I wanted to get from motherhood. I knew this could happen only if I stayed home. But even so, when my son was born, rather than resign from my job, I took a year's leave, after which a job had to be available for me if I wanted it. Maybe I felt an obligation to use my college education. Maybe it was hard to come to terms with how a career can be everything and then become suddenly disposable. Perhaps it was simply easier for my ego to say I was on a leave of absence from a major newspaper than to say I was now "just" a mom. Not that anyone asked. They were too busy smiling at my baby. "Just" a mom—that's laughable when I consider how much work and passion go into a round-the-clock career that changes lives.

Recently I overheard my son tell a friend what I used to do. They spent just six seconds on the topic, but it stopped

"Part of it was that I had and have a financial responsibility to my family. Part of it was ego. I was twenty-seven. Having a child at this stage in my life just wasn't my plan. I thought I'd just keep moving. It never occurred to me I wouldn't 'keep soldiering on,' as my grandmother would say. I was proud of the fact I was going to carry part of the burden. When I thought about excelling at home, well, I just felt I was worth more than that. When I went back, though, I was immediately conflicted. And I have come to the place that I love taking care of my family. I truly love it."

Kim

me in my tracks and unearthed feelings about my identity I thought were pretty well buried. My thoughts on working moms have evolved greatly since my first trip to the delivery room. Yours will too. Let them. And make well-thought-out decisions.

My friend Stacie said she cried the first week of saying good-bye to her son when she left him with the caregiver. Then she and her husband realized tears wouldn't raise a baby, so they became purposeful in maximizing the time they did have together. She couldn't choose not to work, but she could choose her attitude. She was helping her family afford diapers, not French lessons.

"I think if you know you are being the best mother you can be, you can let go of the self-pity or the guilt," she said. "I sang to my baby the entire way home when I picked him up. I didn't waste time."

## What to Look For in Child Care

- **Reputation.** Talk to parents who use the child care center or provider.
- **Qualified staff.** Look for enthusiasm and gentleness. Check on discipline, feeding, and sleeping practices; first aid and CPR training; and staff turnover rates. The American Academy of Pediatrics recommends a 3-to-1 child-staff ratio for babies up to one year old, with a maximum group size of six. The recommended ratio is 4-to-1 for children from twelve to thirty months, with a maximum group size of eight.
- **Safety.** Look for cleanliness in all areas, an emergency plan, and childproofing. Check on the enforcement of sick rules and immunization policies.
- **Visiting encouraged.** You should be able to stop in for a visit unannounced.
- **A set routine.** There should be a schedule, which includes time for rest, play, group and individual activities, snacks, and meals. Ask about the policy for watching TV or videos. Look for the encouragement of creativity and imagination and for age-appropriate toys.
- **A current license.** Check to see if the center is accredited by the National Association for the Education of Young Children. Start with ChildCareAware. org or call 1-800-424-2246.

"I think getting ready to say good-bye had to take a backseat to getting ready—period. We tried not to fly around the house, but you just do. I'd always try to take that extra fifteen seconds to pull it together, remind myself of why I had to go to work, and tell myself that my baby was going to be loved on all day. It helped."

Kristi

Elizabeth, who now works part-time from home with kindergarten twins, agreed. "Now I intentionally take that time to go out on the front porch to look at the roly-poly or other fascinating bugs. That ten-minute investment is everything. You choose to read the book at night. You don't turn on the TV."

To help Katie focus exclusively on her kids in the evenings, she organizes everything else she can in advance. She opens mail daily and near the trash can to avoid a pileup. Grocery shopping happens only once a week. Laundry waits till the weekend. Meals are planned. And two nights a month are reserved for mom, when she can do something she enjoys by herself.

Mornings can be pretty hairy for working parents who have had a particularly hard night with the baby or find spit-up on their dry-clean-only clothes on the way out the door. Trying to fold a load of laundry or pay a couple of bills when you should be getting out the door will only add to your stress. Stay focused on a calm transition. Learn to leave some things undone.

My friend Stephanie remembers life with her first baby: "I did it wrong for a while. I could not get to work on time. I followed Ashley's schedule until I realized I had to set the pace. I had to decide when we started our day."

Stacie's husband, Tim, would drop their son at a cousin's, who then took him to Tim's mom's home for the day. Stacie had a forty-five-minute commute in a different direction, and so they repeated the two-leg process in the evening. Another friend handed her baby girl to a relative at a gas station, as her commute and her relative's home dictated. It's a tough memory for her.

Even if you are fortunate enough to leave baby at home with a caregiver, planning ahead emotionally and logistically will help you get in a groove and be better prepared when that last-minute diaper blowout happens.

Elizabeth recalled being ready to leave for work one morning when one of her twins had a leaky poop, so she changed her and her clothes, and then her brother's, since they wore matching outfits. Then he threw up. "Not necessary," she said in hindsight. "You learn."

Deciding who cares for your child while you work is a highly personal decision that takes time. Consider the takeaways below and on the next page from moms who chose their mother-in-law to care for their new baby.

You can ask every working mom you know what she's done and you still might not hear what's right for *your* family. The good news is if something doesn't work, you can adjust. One friend I know went through four caregivers for her twins before she found the one who has been with the family for five years. Katie went through seven child care situations. Her best advice: be secure in your role as a mom while also being comfortable with someone else loving your children.

At work, mothers quickly learn that they don't shed one hat to wear another. The hats just pile up. If you wait tables, you look at families in a different light. If you teach, your empathy for children—and their parents—expands. Whatever you sell, whomever you serve, you now add to your job

"I couldn't speak my mind about how she cared for my child. And it took away from her being just Grandma because eventually she had to be a disciplinarian. I would feel guilty for not checking in every three hours."

Stephanie

"He got the most love he possibly could have outside of me. That alone mattered more than the stuff we did differently."

Stacie

the perspective of a woman with a child. It's a beautiful thing to have mothers in the workplace. You can relate more fully to co-workers with children too.

Hopefully your work environment and supervisor can adjust to your new role. Tardiness is inevitable once in a while, as are unexpected sick days or leaving at midday to pick up a child who has a fever. The really fun adjustment for those with male bosses is taking breaks to pump milk.

"I had a boss who was appalled I would have to retreat three times a day to pump," my friend Stephanie remembers. "I had a dream job, and this was a whole new challenge I had to face. The flow of your day, your time, it's not your own, whether you're at home or work."

*Before* you return to work, talk to your supervisor about your need to pump milk. Especially if that boss is male, be straightforward but not graphic. He might have a wife or sister and be familiar with your situation, or it may throw him for a loop.

"We finally got off the formal daycare path and went to find a grandma. We wanted our kids to feel like family never left. And we wanted warm meals and hugs and kisses over major early childhood development. It's different for everyone, but just figuring that out was a blessing to us.

My mistake was thinking my influence couldn't be felt until I was home. I thought my nanny was the expert. I wished she would call me at work. I wished I'd said, 'Please talk a lot about mommy and daddy.' I never asked her to. As a new mom, you lack confidence and think, Everybody knows my child better than me. I didn't trust my instincts and lean on God enough. It was a tough time that existed quietly in my soul for a long time."

Kim

## Making It Work

**Plan for the morning the night before.** Choose clothes for both you and baby. Have your bag and/or breast pump packed or even in the car. Set out breakfast. Taking care of the "stuff" in advance will leave you more energy for the emotion of the morning and the unexpected happenings.

**Get up early.** Getting yourself ready first frees you to focus on baby's needs and bonding with him. Consider playing soft music instead of the morning news to set a peaceful tone.

**Have an honest conversation with your boss in advance of returning to work.** Discuss any changes to your routine you may have to make to accommodate pumping, daycare hours, and any other responsibilities. Don't use this conversation for an emotional dump. Stick to the facts.

**If using an individual caregiver, spend time together before your first day of work.** Have her over for lunch. Talk about what happens when she or baby is sick, how often you plan to check in, and what happens when she runs late or you do. You can't anticipate everything that might come up, but establishing an honest rapport can save you angst later on.

**Remember that you and your husband are partners.** Make your marital relationship a priority—even if it means staying up late to check in with one another. Share your feelings on being a working mom. Listen to his feelings on leaving the baby with a caregiver as well. And then share things that have nothing to do with work or baby!

**Discuss household duties with your spouse.** Decide together who will do what and the things you can let go, as you find your new routine.

**Cultivate a support system of moms who have been where you are.** Some MOPS groups (MOPS.org) meet in the evening. At these meetings you can ask other moms what worked for them and what didn't.

Determine where you can do it, how long your breaks can be and how frequent, and where you can store the milk. You'll need enough storage containers to make it through the day and a cooler for transporting milk home safely. It's always a good idea to have an extra shirt at work in case your breasts leak, as well as a small blanket for privacy and a do-not-disturb sign for the door. One of my workplaces hung a big "Got Milk?" poster on the door of a room deemed the "lactation lounge" because of a number of new moms in the office. You may not want to be that on display, but it certainly normalized for the rest of the office a routine happening in the lives of several women.

As in all things maternal, your attitude makes a big difference in pumping at work. Being relaxed encourages the letdown reflex and will get you back to your desk quicker. Looking at a picture of your baby helps too. If you make

## Home Work

### Reaping the Benefits while Getting Something Done

Welcoming baby to a home that's also a home office brings its own challenges. Whether it's you or your husband—or both—who manage a career from home, the key to a productive rhythm is setting up a space and a routine that lets you enjoy the perks of being together.

Just because you are at home doesn't mean you can work and parent *at the same time*. Especially as your baby grows, you'll need to consider in-home caregiving, even if you're there.

Here are some things to consider:

- Use a headset with a quickly accessible mute button.
- Schedule important calls during nap time or a designated time when baby is out with someone else on errands or play dates.
- Plan lunch together as a family.
- Be honest with your clients or customers to diffuse the stress of always feeling you need silence when you are on the phone. There's no reason to hide that you're in a home office, as millions are these days.
- Use earplugs if you need to.
- Close the door when you need to.
- Be respectful of the job being done and don't poke your head in on a whim and break your spouse's concentration.
- Save those old keyboards! Soon enough your baby will be pounding away with you.
- When you're off, be off. Setting limits on your work hours is even more important when you have little ones to love.
- Be realistic. Where you live, the size of your family, or the nature of your job may make a home office unworkable.

pumping as normal and personal as brushing your teeth, then it will be. If you make a big deal of toting milk around or being "ready to burst" or misuse your pumping breaks, the attention you get may not be positive.

Remember, all mothers continually reassess what they are doing, why they are doing it, and how they can best parent their children. If you have children and are working outside the home, you have two careers. This makes it all the more important that you find your rhythm.

## LIVING ON BABY TIME

### My Rattled Daze

1. I work because . . .
   I don't work because . . .
2. Does my husband support my working outside of the home? Have we discussed how we will divide up the household responsibilities so that my working is realistic?
3. When and how will I reassess how staying at home or being a working parent is going? What does a successful rhythm look like for my family?

# 8

## Permission Granted

### *Time for Mom*

Being a new mom is at once exhilarating and stifling. Knowing someone is fully dependent on you is one thing, but now you are dependent on someone else too—if you want to go anywhere without your child. This is definitely not baby shower conversation.

It first hit me when my son was five months old and I needed an emergency root canal. I was hurting so bad and still I had to make the calls and impose on someone else so I could have the pleasure of having my tooth drilled. While I was grateful for my sister's willingness and ability to take a half day off work—my husband was out of town—I remember feeling pretty humbled by my limits, and more than a little ornery too.

Over time I think moms learn to work with the reality of needing child care and needing time for themselves. You get creative. You appreciate a fifteen-minute errand you get to do alone. And if you're like me, you take showers that are

"If you have a bad week at work you can say, 'Friday's coming.' When you are a new mom, there is no weekend. It doesn't stop. So I started to grab my weekend throughout the week. Fifteen minutes at a time to do something for me. One nap at a time. If I couldn't get a real break, I tried to find the mental time away."

Noell

too long and too hot, soaking in the solitude and steaming away the world.

When my friend Angela's first son was a baby, as soon as her husband got home, she'd often take off for Starbucks for an hour. She'd sit, drink coffee, and read a newspaper. I'm not sure if I was jealous or judgmental, but I wondered why she had to leave her home. When I had my third child, I finally understood. Coincidentally, that's also when I started drinking coffee!

"You ask yourself, *Is he safe?* Then you do what you need to do. We can't be replaced as mothers, but it's okay to leave and to want to leave. You need to be rejuvenated," Angela says.

Angela also dealt with the monotony of care giving by approaching it as she approached her careers—trying to be the best she could. She'd research and read on child development, she became a trained presenter of the Love and Logic parenting/teaching method, and she was always looking for experiences to enhance motherhood and childhood for her boys. She looked to vary her rhythm, as that made life—just like music—much more enjoyable.

The more children you have, the more assertive you have to be about getting time to nurture yourself—or just get that badly needed haircut. I've thought about going to my husband with a permission slip to sign, to highlight how it feels as though I have to get permission to do something—anything—alone. But I think he gets it. Once I took nine months to use a spa gift certificate he gave me one Mother's Day. He *gave* it to me, and still I felt guilty going off to use it.

63

"I kept thinking, *If I can just get through this time nursing*. I would pray for the sun to come up again and hope I could do another day. I lost myself. I grew up watching *Little House on the Prairie*. Caroline Ingalls—that was going to be me. Baking, being all calm and loving and welcoming dad home with a hug, family life being everything and my kids loving me.

"I didn't count on being so tired I couldn't remember if I fed the baby. It was hard to find glory, or validation, in what I was doing. But it happened. I started to find purpose and joy in my family."

Noell

I wish I'd started earlier making regular time for me because it does get easier when you realize how revitalizing it is.

Women have to be judicious about choosing their escapes. There is much daytime television out there that isn't healthy for your brain or your body—not talking "Oprah" here—but it's a quick fix when you're stuck in the house and want to "go" somewhere else. We all love a *People* magazine once in a while, but motherhood is for the long haul. Losing yourself in soap operas or celebrity news doesn't nourish your soul. Neither does food or alcohol or shopping.

As you think about getting "permission" to take care of yourself, I want to also give you permission to have mixed feelings about this new world order.

Parenting is hard the first time. You make mistakes. You drown in ignorance. You wonder how the women on the darn commercials have bright complexions and spotless floors for their babies to crawl on. And you might wonder if this is what you signed up for. Maybe you are waiting to feel the warm fuzzies of being a mom that you expected would come automatically.

Vanessa struggled with the lack of an immediate connection to her second son—even more surprising to her because he was indeed her second. She attributes the delay to the five days he fought jaundice, under special lights so that she couldn't even cuddle him after a feeding. Add that to a miscarriage between children, and Vanessa realized this baby started life as more of a medical project than a person.

This is the case for many new moms who have suffered infertility before having a baby. They are used to healing from—or distancing themselves altogether from—another negative pregnancy test. There's support and attention when you are struggling to achieve and maintain a pregnancy, but when you are a new mom, you are on your own, considered "normal" all of a sudden.

You have to share your feelings, wherever they originated and whatever they are. Don't add to your stress or disappointment by stuffing them down deep and hoping they'll disappear. My experience is that just speaking an issue out loud can help lessen its intensity in your heart.

"It's okay to say to your friends and family, 'I'm not enjoying myself right now.' I totally thought I couldn't complain because I was home," one friend said. "This is what I wanted. But in the beginning you think it's going to be more satisfying. I had to talk that out."

Give it a few months. When your baby is six weeks old, make an effort to get in a rhythm, a routine. Reach out to connect with other moms, and keep watching that baby. Seeing those smiles—the early ones you know are meant only for you—will change your relationship to your child and to your job as a mom. Suddenly you realize you aren't

"People knew we had struggled with infertility; they knew how much we wanted this child. To assure that the whole experience was perfect, I felt like I needed to love everything. I bargained with God and said, 'Give me a baby, and I'll be the perfect mom.' I had it in my head how it should be. I wasn't prepared for the imperfections. My life had been on schedule. I'd always looked for the next goal. Now I didn't know what the goal was."

Liz

alone. There's a little buddy ready to blossom inside those footed jammies.

When my oldest was six months old, I attended one of my first MOPS meetings. It was fall, the leaves were changing, and sitting with other mothers twice a month was changing my perspective on what it meant to be home with a child. After losing two pregnancies, I already knew motherhood was a calling, a privilege. But now I was *seeing* it, by sharing the fun and frustration of the journey with other women.

On the way home from that meeting, though my son was pretty tired after only a brief nap in MOPS child care, something inspired me to take a spontaneous left turn. There was a park I'd been told had awesome fall foliage. I happened to have my camera.

My baby boy adored exploring the crunchy gold carpet I'd set him on. His plaid hat framed a beautiful toothless grin. As I clicked the camera, I started to cry. I knew that every infertility treatment and grieving hour and labor push and sleepless night had been worth it. I needed no permission to be here. I was the mom.

## LIVING ON BABY TIME

*My Rattled Daze*

1. What has surprised me most about becoming a mom?
2. Where would I go and what would I do if I had four hours by myself?
3. Have I given myself permission to get away from my baby? How have I handled the need for child care?

# 9

## Daddy Dish

*Living in Different Daytime Worlds*

"Whadya do today, honey?"

"Well, I put clothes on. Put clothes on the baby. Put more clothes on the baby after she pooped out of that pink thing I like so much. I called my mom but got off the phone because the baby wasn't latching on real well . . .

"I went to the store but got only some of the things on my list because I realized I was leaking and didn't time our outing very well. I unloaded the dishwasher halfway and opened some of the mail. We played patty-cake—I really think she smiled! I made her next doctor's appointment, but I think I might change it since your mom is coming in town. I put those shirts in the car but didn't quite get them to the dry cleaners. You know, the store debacle . . .

"I had plans for making this new thing for dinner, but since I didn't get all the stuff, I decided we'd have burgers instead . . . Ooooh. Forgot to thaw out the meat. Feel like a pizza?"

"So you didn't really do *anything*?"

Hand this book to your husband right now.

Husbands, try never to come home and ask "*What* did you do today?" Chances are, the laundry list of attempts will make you dizzy. Your response, though well-intentioned and even factual, could put your wife over the edge. The better question is "*How* was your day, dear?" That way, if she didn't *do* a darn thing to completion, she doesn't have to be reminded. Okay, hand the book back.

When you are intently looking for your new rhythm as a mom, it's easy to forget things have changed quite a bit for dad too. He's operating as his former self at work on his current sleep budget, which is likely tight. He's trying to navigate your fluctuating sense of purpose, mom-confidence, and sleep deficit. And he's also trying to use the limited hours he has at home to establish himself as daddy in the eyes of the newest member of your household.

Even though he probably leaves every day for work, it's a new rhythm for him too. Maybe you're thinking, *No way. Nothing has changed for him, and my life is upside down.* Ask him. Gently. But don't do it during the workday.

I'm extremely guilty of picking up the phone during the day when I have a thought I desperately want to share. He's my best friend and daddy to my crazy crew—of course it's him I want to call. But he's also employed, with co-workers usually within earshot of his cell phone. So I'm trying to be more judicious.

We've developed an understanding that if I call and he can't talk, he simply says, "Call ya back," and hangs up without waiting for me to respond. When I was alone with baby, wanting to share something he did—something monumental I'm sure, like toot—I didn't take well to being cut short. But of course that was selfish. And now I'm the one who often cuts him short during a daytime call as chaos reigns around me or I don't have an extra thirty seconds before needing to get someone somewhere. I'm so grateful for the times my husband has let me ramble, as when our middle son emptied a bag of flour on top of his head, and I just had to describe the scene in great detail.

Ask your husband about the rhythm of his day, when it's best to touch base, and when it's not a good time. You may think you know but you're probably experiencing more things than ever that you want to share, and that might cloud your judgment as you reach for the phone.

Some of my friends practice "couch time." For fifteen minutes after husband gets home, they sit and recap the day, with a rule of no interruptions. Both get heard, but the idea here is deeper: mom and dad's relationship is sacred, and this is sacred time. Three increasingly vocal sons, who adore attacking their dad as soon as he arrives, make this tough for us. Perhaps if we'd begun doing it with one sleeping newborn, it wouldn't be so hard now. It's crucial for your kids to see you giving your marriage top priority.

During the day, I've been known to actually keep a list of what I want to tell my husband. It prevents verbal diarrhea on my part when he walks in the door, and I can wait until it's quiet enough to share because I'm not worried about something slipping out of my head. When Todd is out of town, our kids keep a daddy box that gets filled with treasures, school papers, and assorted things we want to share. And when he gets back, it's great fun to roll it out. This comes in handy, especially when we are in different time zones and phone time is tough. Sometimes I put my own thoughts in there with the kids' stuff.

However you do it, the point is to respect each other's evolving rhythms and keep on communicating.

## LIVING ON BABY TIME

### My Rattled Daze

1. What time of day are my husband and I most likely to have a productive conversation? When are we least likely to communicate effectively?

2. How can I better communicate my feelings and my needs to my husband?
3. How can I encourage a good relationship between my husband and our child?
4. How can I let my husband know that even when I'm busy with the baby, our relationship is my top priority?

# Making Sweet Music

## The Changing Melodies of Motherhood

"Drums." For years on my self-indulgent Christmas lists, that's what this little girl wrote. Odd for a girl, odder perhaps for a girlie girl like me. But there was something I loved about the way two hands could work separately and yet together. A song could start with a single beat, and then the song could swallow the beat, but it was still there underneath, giving life to the music. Who doesn't love drummers? They are the mysterious men in the background, at least usually men anyway, but you can always look forward to their moment in the spotlight, because there's never a wasted second. What energy! I always thought. What coordination!

I never got those drums—and no apologies necessary, Mom and Dad. I understand why. But these days I might as well be a drummer, the energetic, hopefully coordinated, multitasking, behind-the-scenes drummer in this band we call a family. My quest is to create a rhythm that drives us forward. It may be even sometimes, unsteady at others, but it's ours.

You'll find your rhythm as a mom. The music may seem chaotic right now. It is. And just when you think you hear sweet stability, the song will change. You'll have to adjust what you do and when and how. Raising children is a series of new songs, and you are a composition in the works too. Just remember, you're not on stage alone. Love your band and keep on drumming. Here's to making the music that's right for you.

# Part 2

# Your Body after Baby

# Introduction

*We're in This Together*

She sat refreshed after a very necessary shower, her oversized rocker moving gently. Through a picture window she could see snow falling from the gray sky. Holding a new baby couldn't have felt more right, more cozy, more miraculous.

In his sleep he lifted a tiny hand and grabbed her finger. "I am home," he seemed to say.

"I am home," she breathed, glancing at the stack of hospital discharge papers and freebies littering the kitchen table. "Now what?"

That perfect moment is etched forever on my heart. The baby I hoped for, prayed for, and waited for was finally in my arms! No one told me that in the days to follow, the euphoria would fade. There were certainly times of unspeakable joy but also unspeakable physical and emotional realities that left me feeling pretty bewildered. I didn't know how to talk about them.

Bleeding, cramping, feeling exhausted, being sore up here and sore down there, starving—but someone else's appetite now coming first. One day everyone is showering a pregnant woman with questions and advice, holding doors open for her, satisfying her cravings. The next day there's a little person outranking his mom's needs at every turn. A life-giving, taut belly has turned to mush, just like the sleep-deprived brain in the same body.

Did you miss the hospital pamphlet on that too?

On the pages that follow, we will seek to identify some of the stealth issues of the heart, mind, and body you might encounter and be unprepared for after bringing a baby home. The "we" I'm referring to is dozens of moms and mom medical professionals who have been there, moms who wish they'd known some things earlier, moms who wish they'd shared more with their friends and family and not felt so isolated, moms who loved this crazy period in their lives and don't want you to go it alone.

Our hope is that you'll gain a new understanding of the challenges you face, see that you are indeed normal, and learn ways to baby *yourself* so you can be at your best as you embark on the privilege of parenting.

# 10

## Whose Body Is This?

### *Navigating and Accepting Change*

After you've had a baby, you don't come home from the hospital the same person who checked in. Whether you delivered vaginally or via cesarean section, in thirty minutes or two days, you must recover. And that's when the real labor begins.

As unique as your birth story was, so will be your road of recovery. Some women bounce back quickly, while others take weeks. Don't beat yourself up if you can't shake that cruddy feeling. *And don't compare yourself with others.* That will get you nowhere but frustrated fast. While people tend to pepper a new mom with questions: "How's the baby doing? How's she sleeping?" I always try to ask how *mom* is feeling. No one is holding *her*, feeding *her* on a schedule, or easing *her* into soft, new pajamas. But maybe we should!

It's been my experience that women feel they can share only the socially acceptable parts of life after baby with most other women. Usually they stick to the sleep challenges. But there's so much more. We'll get to the emotional ride shortly, but first, some honest thoughts on the gory after the glory of having a baby.

## Bleeding

You knew there would be blood involved in childbirth. You may not have realized that *mom* gets to wear a diaper afterward too. The discharge, called *lochia*, is heavier with a vaginal birth than a C-section—having had both, I can vouch for that. It's tissue from the lining of your womb and should turn from bright red to pink or brown and be about finished by the time you have your six-week, post-baby checkup, if not before. But it can feel like it goes on forever. The humongous pads provided in the hospital might seem bulky and bothersome—very institutional—but use them. Take home the extras. You'll change them often enough in the beginning not to care about anything but coverage; plus, six weeks of pads gets expensive. Take home the sexy mesh underwear too. Use it. Take it. Trash it.

When you are breast-feeding, your uterus contracts, and it's likely you will feel gushes of blood when you stand up after, if not during, nursing. You should err on the side of changing your pads too often, just to be ready for these times. Remember that dad will have no idea what's going on inside you as you attempt to feed the baby. I always felt a little reminder was in order. I'm not sure what I wanted him to say, but I'm pretty sure he didn't say it. Really, how could he understand? Still I longed for his empathy.

I said we were going to be honest, right? Well here goes. After my third son was born by C-section two months early, I was hooked up to a catheter, some blood pressure socks, an IV, a pain ball for my incision, and I'm not sure what else. With two young boys at home, my husband was pretty much homebound, and I was pretty much alone. If the white board they use as a pain scale had been within reach, I might have hurled it across the room. I was trying desperately to find a comfortable position for my stapled stomach and get some rest, and suddenly I felt like I had to go to the bathroom—right away. I was like a creature from a bad sci-fi movie, lumbering across the room with all my wires and machinery and three-day-dirty hair. When I managed to pull down and sit down, I thought I would pass out from the pain and loneliness of the moment.

And then my uterus dropped in the toilet. Or so I thought. By then I'd pulled the cord, and a nurse was trying to assess the source of my tears. She assured me that it wasn't my uterus and told me I'd passed a blood clot the size of a grapefruit. Lovely!

I share this for a couple of reasons, neither of which is to frighten you. If you don't feel right about what your body is doing, don't suffer in silence. Call the doctor. Clots are common at home too, though usually not that big. But if you aren't sure, ask. Here's the bigger picture: there are moments after having a baby, in the hospital and at home, that you feel desperately alone, rocked by the physical trauma you've just undergone and the ripple effects it has on your body and spirit. Personally, I think it's preparation for the job ahead. Think how glass is tested and twisted in fire to become beautiful art. I think the first months after the birth of our baby mold us, cultivating our empathy for those who suffer, making us into mothers. It can be a gut-wrenching process, literally.

Not long after that experience, I was comforting my five-year-old on the bathroom floor during a bout of the stomach flu. This time I was the nurse, but I remembered well the tears that come from feeling like your insides are falling out. And I hope I never forget.

## Ouch

It hurts to pee. If you delivered vaginally, you will probably have pain caused by stretching, tearing, or cutting. My hospital had a can of Dermoplast, an anesthetic spray, waiting to soothe. It helped (and it works on cuts and scrapes, so I moved it to the kids' first-aid kit when I'd recovered). The hospital also recommended using a squirt bottle of warm water on the vaginal area to dilute the stinging potential of urine. I dreaded how much it hurt to pee, so I waited until the last second. The squirt bottle doesn't help when it's not ready and waiting or the water is cold! But if you can "plan ahead," and bite your lip, it helps.

If you are afraid to pee, imagine your delight when it's time for number two! Hopefully in the hospital you were given a stool softener to make that experience bearable. Drink water—lots of water.

If you received an episiotomy, a surgical cut to enlarge the baby's exit path, the pain might be a little more intense, but it will end. Prolific mom-and-baby author Ann Douglas once said of her own episiotomy: "I can still remember how gingerly I had to sit for weeks after the fact. I perfected the art of sitting at a forty-five-degree angle on one bum cheek because it was too painful to sit in my regular position" (WebMD live interview,

## Feeling Low
## Down Low

### Good Advice

Ice packs, best early on.
Pain reliever, as directed by a doctor. Do not take aspirin if you are breast-feeding.
Frequent pad-changing.
Warm-water squirt bottle while you pee.
Squeeze your cheeks together as you sit down.
Limit how long you sit still.
Witch hazel compresses.
Sitz baths: shallow warm-water soaks.
Take stool softener as directed and drink plenty of water; don't strain with bowel movements.
Always call a doctor with increased pain or swelling or if you run a fever.

August 26, 2003). She advises a hemorrhoid cushion or extra pillows on hand to help assist with a comfortable sitting position. There were two words the nurses used a lot that I'd never heard before childbirth: *sitz bath*. Easy enough, right? You just *sit* in the bath. Well, apparently a sitz bath is a plastic tub that fits over the toilet and can be filled with a few inches of warm water. Sit for twenty minutes and get relief. I had three children before I knew what the tub was for. I thought it was for toting home all your stuff. They should hand out vocabulary lists with those home instructions.

The second term that caught me clueless was *witch hazel*. It's an herbal remedy that dries and cleanses the skin, an astringent produced from steaming the twigs of a shrub. All you *need* to know is that drugstores sell witch hazel wipes that are very soothing in helping heal your baby exit. And later you can use them on other sores, bruises, swelling, eczema, shaving cuts, insect bites, poison ivy, sunburns, and blisters. Not a bad purchase.

Witch hazel is also helpful for hemorrhoids. *Sigh.* Yes, another lovely reward for carrying another person around for nine months. Hemmies are a frequent result of pushing during childbirth and the pressure we exert when we feel constipated. It's like walking around with highly sensitive grapes between your legs. Only one thing made me feel better when I developed one of these lovelies while pregnant with my second child—empathy. A good friend happened to call me just as I was getting off the phone with a nurse who had advised me, "Just push it back in." I was in tears. I decided to come clean and tell my friend the reason for my sorrow. "Susan," she said, "remember a few months ago when you asked if I was tired or upset? You said I seemed a little sad? *That* was why." She went on to share her travails. It was only then that I knew I'd survive. Beautiful, intelligent, seemingly together people get them too, and live to walk again at a normal pace.

A few more words on dealing with pain. Everyone has a different threshold for discomfort. I know mine expanded

> "Those first weeks seemed like a dream world, so fuzzy. I didn't expect the pain."
>
> Lynda

greatly after I had kids. Either that or I finally realized that complaining wasn't going to make me feel better! But if you hurt, you hurt. Take your doctor's advice on medication. You are not weak because you need medicinal relief. Also, seek distraction. If nursing the baby is uncomfortable in the beginning, as it often is, have a movie on low volume or play some soothing music or thumb through a magazine. Slowed, focused, and deep breathing also became a great friend of mine in recovering from C-sections. Sometimes pain leads to frustration, which leads to stress . . . and then you find yourself tied up in knots both physically and mentally. I also tended to find a mantra to repeat when I was feeling great discomfort. "This is only a phase" or "Thank you, God, for this baby" helped me get perspective in the midst of the hurt.

Time is your friend here. Take one step at a time. No one is timing your recovery the way they time your contractions. Get rid of the panting and breathe deeply. You're no longer in a sprint; now it's a marathon.

### C-ing Is Believing

Could there possibly be a more helpless feeling than lying pregnant and naked on an operating table, being shaved and

> "I craved going to the chiropractor for a massage during those first six months. I think the combination of recuperating from the C-section, breast weight, feeding and holding the baby was a difficult surprise on my muscles."
>
> Lisa

drugged because your baby, with a dropping heart rate, is about to be swiftly delivered from your abdomen? I knew plenty of women who had had C-sections and seemed nonchalant about it. So I thought there was something wrong with me that, months later, my mind kept replaying the *fuzzy* trauma of my own experience. I didn't talk about it, but every time I closed my eyes, it was there.

Surgery is no small deal. Our bodies have to recover, and I'd suggest our minds do too. Perhaps you were unprepared for a C-section and disappointed not to finish out a vaginal delivery. Don't let anyone try to whisk away your feelings with one-liners. Yes, the most important thing is that your baby is healthy and here to cherish, but you need to work through your feelings in your own way, your own time.

Even if you were expecting a C-section, the bright lights of the operating room—and the dim memories anesthesia can

### The Skin You're In

**DO...**

Drink plenty of water to help flush out the toxins of anesthesia and hormones.

Avoid excessive caffeine and soda pop, as it dehydrates and is bad for nursing.

Try alternating hair products to give your hair a boost, but don't expect anything to stop hair loss after giving birth.

Use an astringent to help with oozing pores.

Take warm rather than hot showers and use a moisturizer just after getting out.

Exercise when you are ready. Working up a sweat is good for you!

**DON'T...**

Waste your money in search of an instant over-the-counter solution to skin woes.

Try to open sores or pimples to get the problem "out." Let them heal on their own.

Hesitate to ask for help. Ask your esthetician or hairdresser for substitute products.

cause—can be quite rattling. I kept asking my husband to recount detail after detail for me. I don't even think I knew how fuzzy my memories were until weeks later. Ask your hubby while his are still clear!

And then there's the big achy zipper in your bikini line. Sleeping will be tricky. Prop lots of pillows around you to protect your wound. I found coughing even trickier. Who knew that clearing a slight throat tickle could be so painful? Again, positioning a pillow across your tummy helps. The incision takes four to six weeks to heal; the abdominal wall muscles may take a few months before they are fully healed.

Don't keep looking at your incision. It *will* look and feel better, but early on, it may seem like a purple mess, and bending forward hurts. Motherhood insists that you learn to look at the sunny side of dreary situations, so you might as well start now. It's a battle scar. It's an excuse not to wear a bikini again. Heck, it's an easier way to one day explain to your kids where babies come from. You now have a PG visual aid.

Things we wish we had known? I would have had my husband's hand present to squeeze when the staples were taken out of my incision. For some, it's no big deal, but for me that brief procedure was miserable. It also surprised me that my scar would remain numb in many spots for a long time. A larger issue is this: when doctors and home instructions say to limit your lifting, stair climbing, and exertion, you should. Many women get bursts of energy and think back-to-normal is one load of laundry away. And then they collapse in a puddle of exhaustion because they've done too much too fast. Slow down.

It's worth mentioning that just as you may not realize the major-surgery implications of a C-section, your husband may not either. He might be expecting you to do more than you can, especially if you are trying to! Share with him the instructions that you brought home from the hospital and connect with him regularly on how you're feeling.

## Wetting the Bed

Waking up in a wet bed can be a problem too, and we're not talking about the baby here. Night sweats can happen because of the major hormonal changes your body is experiencing. With each child I had, somehow I forgot that I'd wake up in a pool of perspiration, my sheets and pajamas very damp. The first time it happened, I thought my breasts had sprung a leak.

Not much to do here but know that it's a brief phenomenon. Keep a clean T-shirt handy, and ask your husband to change the sheets before they start to smell.

This is as good a place as any to say this: *shower often.* Every bit of ickiness you feel after delivery, after a sweaty night, after a day of nursing, after getting spit up on—all can be helped with a good shower and the fresh start it engenders. Just don't let your C-section incision remain in the shower's path too long early on. Now is a great time to use that sweet-smelling body wash and lotion you've been saving under your sink. As one friend says, "I didn't even need to do my hair or put on makeup. I just felt so much better when I was clean."

## Skin and Hair

I wanted to lose weight; instead, I lost hair. I wanted to be full of wisdom, but only my pores were full—of gunk. I wish I'd known how temporary these changes are, but when there's so much going on with your body at once, it's hard to imagine a day when you'll actually enjoy looking in the mirror again.

Both breast-feeding and bottle-feeding mothers lose hair. It grows like a weed during pregnancy, and then it falls out at around three months and up to a year after delivery. A little whisk of the drain with a tissue each day will save you buying a bottle of declogger. Little tufts of hair will sprout again, in some places giving you the look of a child gone wild with scissors. I tried a lot of different shampoos through and after pregnancy, hoping to find the one that would greet my raging hormones with salon-fresh manageability. You might try a product recommended for making your hair feel thicker. But time helps the most.

Stephanie, a hair stylist and mother of three, told me women often impetuously try to do something radical to their hair for a lift of their spirits. "You still feel so fat and ugly and you want a cosmetic change, when what you really need is a change from within," she said. Remember, short hair is less hair to deal with, but if it's a new style for you, it might take just as much time to deal with.

When one of her children was a baby, Stephanie decided spontaneously to get her hair cut at a chain hair salon she'd never been to before. With her hair cut up to her ears in some places due to some bad communication, she left bawling. At home, her husband told her she looked like a pumpkin. Shortly after her bad hair cut, while nursing, Stephanie reached back to what used to be her long, thick hair to find only dried spit-up. That sent her running for another cut—this time for practical not emotional reasons. She went to a recommended stylist this time!

"Think it through. Go gradually shorter or gradually with another color. We don't realize how attached we are to our hair," she says. "And a bad hair day can really send you."

Your skin may also go on strike. For me, nowhere was the hormonal shift more evident. I had an unexplained break-out/rash on my trunk through my pregnancies. I wanted to scrub myself raw, but none of my drugstore purchases did a thing to help. The rash would start at twenty weeks and begin to disappear only when my baby was a couple weeks old—a blip on the calendar, but in the midst of pregnancy and new baby, it seemed like forever. No one could see it, but it affected my self-esteem daily, and I don't think I told a single friend. When I changed clothes, I started avoiding the mirror and hiding from my husband. A dermatologist took an inconclusive biopsy and recommended a very gentle soap. No help. My perinatologist said having the baby was the only cure. Guess it was an early lesson that baby changes everything and we can only control so much.

Acne, worrisome spots, and rashes are the most common reasons for dermatologist visits after having a baby, says Dr. Barbara Reed, a clinical professor at the University of Colorado Health Sciences Center. "Most rashes are unexplained," Dr. Reed says. "Everyone always wants to know why they got a rash, but it is very, very rare that we can actually tell you that. Everything seems so urgent and different, but don't panic. It makes things worse." Dr. Reed also advises, "Don't expect things to go away overnight. Most skin problems take at least two weeks to get even a little better."

Stretch marks and varicose veins will take much longer to fade or shrink, though sadly they may never disappear completely. A dermatologist can help you consider your options. Retin A, other vitamin A products, chemical peels, and microdermabrasion may help and can be used, even if you're nursing.

It took nine months for your body to get like this. Give it time to bounce back. Facials and massages can help not only your body but your spirit as well. Most of your concerns will soon be distant memories. Work through one problem at a time, and try not to lump your maladies together lest you feel your entire body is betraying you. Your body isn't the enemy; it grew a child for nine months, and it has earned the right to some tender care.

## YOUR BODY AFTER BABY

*Babying Me*

1. The most challenging physical aspect of having had a baby for me right now is . . .
2. These words describe my body and how I feel about it:
3. Whom have I asked for help or advice? Where might I find answers or relief?

# 11

## Breast-Feeding Bumps

### *Being Someone Else's Refrigerator Isn't Always a Picnic*

Few mothering issues elicit as emotional a response as breast-feeding. Some women adore nourishing children from their bodies. They love the closeness and dread the end of that chapter of baby's life. Others dread nearly every feeding. They never feel at ease using their body in the process.

According to the National Women's Health Information Center, breastmilk provides the most complete nutrition for your baby, is easier than formula to digest, promotes proper weight gain, and may even lead to children being less over-

> "For me it's always been a gift to my babies. But it's almost like God's gift to me. It's precious time with them. I'm able to feed them and keep them going. How rewarding is that?"
>
> Tania

"I never knew nursing was physical and emotional for a mom. If someone asked me how I was in those early months, I think my answer depended on how well the baby ate that day—if we were clicking. One day I realized my mood had to be my own and that she wasn't responsible for how I felt about nursing. She was learning too."

Sarah

weight later in life. For moms, nursing uses up extra calories, making it easier to lose the pounds of pregnancy, and lowers the risk of breast and ovarian cancer.

But whatever you know intellectually about nursing, it's normal to be caught off guard physically as you get going. How do you prepare for the sensation of a newborn gnawing at your chest, a lactation expert handling you, or the sight of your body spraying milk four feet away? To be honest, I looked forward to nursing, but just hearing the word *nipple* spoken over and over made me a little uneasy. As one friend put it, "Paying that much attention to any part of my body was a new experience."

It may take a little while before your experience of breast-feeding goes from surprising to rewarding. The contracting of your uterus as you feed your baby is, at moments, an intense cramping. But it's short-lived. Engorgement is what happens when your breasts fill with milk. A woman can go from fretting that she will never have milk come in to becoming several bra sizes bigger in just hours. Even well-endowed women can be in awe of their ballooning cleavage. The achy discomfort of engorgement may require patience and warm compresses as your body and your baby work together to determine how much milk is needed for each feeding.

How a woman's body "performs" is probably going to determine in part what appeal breast-feeding has for her. If there is a good milk supply, a comfortable latch from baby to nipple, and limited soreness, it makes a difference. How a woman views her body also plays a role. The practice is universal, but it's also unique to each woman.

"It's invasive, private, maybe a little awkward, but I loved the baby being that close to me," Lisa said. "That's what kept me going."

My friend Denise said she never realized nursing would hurt her nipples at the beginning, "but then I don't even like to pluck my eyebrows!" she said.

I was lucky. I enjoyed nursing, and it came pretty naturally for my kids and me. Even my little two-and-a-half-pounder was a quick learner. I pumped on full power, never got mastitis, nursed each child for nine to fourteen months, and at the end kept telling myself "just one more time" for many more times. It felt natural. I felt needed.

I have also seen my babies sneeze boogies on my breasts; had a houseguest pick up a stray, *used* nursing pad that had fallen out; pumped in a moving car many times; and occasionally felt uncomfortably scrutinized in public for giving my kids the recommended nutritional start in life—even though I was well-covered. It's not always easy.

The decision to breast-feed is your call. Just don't make the call to stop too early. Our entire life changes when we bring baby home. It's amazing he doesn't start crawling immediately to get away from our racing heart and shaky nerves. *Breast-feeding is uncomfortable in the beginning, and you*

"My breasts were hard, huge melons. I'll never forget the sight. How are you supposed to nurse? I had to stand under hot water to help soften them. When I was nursing, I hated having my boobs out. I'm modest, so I'd always be in another room and alone all the time. I didn't feel like it was a bonding experience with my baby. I breast-fed for two weeks and detested every moment. A friend of mine mentioned pumping. It was my savior, since for me the most important thing about nursing was the nutritional benefit. By pumping and using a bottle, my baby received the nutrition and I avoided the embarrassment. My second son and I had a totally different beginning. I pumped the whole time."

Angela

"The first time around, I wish I would have had someone come to my own house—not the hospital room—to help me out. I just got so confused about the whole nursing thing, how much, how often, when do you wake them. You don't realize that getting stressed out decreases your milk. I really tried to put on a happy face, but I just didn't love it."

Jenn

*will not get the hang of it in a week.* Your baby is changing enormously, and no two days may seem alike. Nursing changes again when your colostrum, your initial offering to the baby, changes to actual milk during baby's first week of life. It changes the first time you eat something your baby reacts to. It changes when your baby goes through a growth spurt and seems to eat nonstop. It changes with her first immunizations. It changes the first time you are up in the middle of the night and feeding isn't the comfort your child is seeking. Try not to lump each circumstance into a nursing-is-too-hard phenomenon. Take one thing at a time *and call those lactation specialists.* Yes, they can come on strong in the hospital, but you were extra-sensitive and all you wanted to do was hold that tiny new mushy person while he slept. Lactation experts have solved countless problems, and they

### Got Milk?

Lagging milk production can frustrate moms. Contact your obstetrician or pediatrician before taking anything, but consider the following for maximizing milk output.

- Keep on a regular schedule with nursing and/or pumping.
- Drink lots of water.
- Watch your diet and make sure you are taking in the recommended 2,500 calories a day.
- Get rest. Yes, it's tough, but it's essential.
- Assess your stress level. Breasts attached to an uptight mom don't work as well.

want to help you give breast-feeding your best shot. (If the hospital where you delivered doesn't provide such help, call the La Leche League at 1-877-4-LALECHE or visit www .lllusa.org to find support in your area.)

My friend Stacia's milk didn't come in for days. Every day she was on the phone with lactation help from the hospital where she delivered. They suggested she add Ovaltine to the milk she drank, because the malt could help. They reminded her to drink lots of water. Together, they waited.

"If it hadn't been for those ladies and my mom, I might have quit," she said. "I went on to nurse for eight months."

### Coming to a Crossroads

Many moms speak of a breast-feeding crossroads they face. It may come at any time, but it brings a moving forward—a comfort level with nursing finally met or an end to nursing efforts. Women stop nursing for different reasons at different stages of baby's life. In the first month or two, baby may not be gaining adequate weight or may not be latching on properly and therefore causing sore spots. At three to eight months, going back to work is tough if the employer is not comfortable with a woman pumping her milk, providing neither the time nor place to do it. At six to nine months,

"Grace was losing a lot of weight in the beginning, and they wanted me to supplement her with formula. I felt so rejected. I had milk but she wasn't taking it, and it made me not like her. I felt so unloved by her, even though I knew I was being irrational. Then one day it was explained to me that when she was nursing forty-five minutes on each side, she got burned out and tired, and the formula was coming without as much effort so she'd take that. I just didn't know what I was doing. I used to be happy to pump so someone else could feed her; then I began not wanting to share her. I got that attachment you hear about, just not at the beginning."

Lynda

"I wish someone had told me that underwire bras can increase your chances of mastitis. I was having a fever, sick to my stomach, and still trying to tell myself, No, nothing's wrong with me. Mastitis can definitely make you want to quit nursing, but it doesn't have to."

Jennifer

those new baby teeth can put the brakes on breast-feeding for some moms.

Sometimes nursing moms automatically connect bouts of fussiness to nursing and get discouraged—probably far more often than there is an actual food sensitivity at the root of the crying. Yes, there are foods that can affect the milk and cause a baby's fussiness, but every mom-baby combination is different, so there isn't one list of "don'ts" to follow. You may want to consider whether there's a family history of food allergies and eat everything in moderation. Chocolate, cow's milk products, and cabbage are common offenders, but many babies handle these just fine. Friends say they had to stay away from oniony salsa. A baby's fussiness that is not accompanied by other symptoms and calms with more frequent nursing is probably not food related. If a breast-fed baby is sensitive to a certain food, she may cry inconsolably for long periods or sleep little and wake suddenly, upset. Other signs of a food allergy include rash, hives, eczema, sore bottom, wheezing or asthma, congestion or coldlike symptoms, red and itchy eyes, vomiting, constipation and/or diarrhea, or green stools containing mucus or blood. Since it can take many days for a food to be completely eliminated from mom's body, sorting out the offending food takes patience. Lactation pros and your pediatrician will help.

Mastitis, a painful inflammation of the breast caused by infection, can be the nursing stumbling block. A woman may not know she has it until she's miserable. Usually you start to hurt in one area of your breast. Maybe it's red or warm to the touch. You may feel achy, like you have the flu. But sleep-

## Whoa Baby!

### Making It through Mastitis

*What it is.* An inflammation of the breast caused by an infection. When milk builds up because of a missed feeding or not being emptied from the breast, it can leak into breast tissue, which can then become swollen and easily infected. Cracked nipples can also allow infection-causing bacteria to get in.

*What you'll feel.* Fever, chills, body aches, exhaustion, and the infected area will feel warm. More advanced symptoms include swollen lymph nodes in the armpit nearest the infected breast, increased heart rate, and/or a hard, painful lump, which could be an abscess.

*What you'll see.* A red area on your breast.

*What to do.* See your doctor, who is likely to prescribe an antibiotic. Take the full course. Keep nursing—it usually helps! Get more rest, drink more fluids, and use cold packs on the painful breast. As your doctor advises, take acetaminophen for pain and ibuprofen to reduce inflammation. Change nursing pads regularly to avoid future infection.

*What not to do.* Don't get discouraged! You can make it through this usually brief pitfall and can continue nursing successfully. Don't wear your nursing bra too tight and don't wear an underwire bra. Don't skip feeding or pumping sessions.

*How to breast-feed.* Try a warm, wet washcloth over the affected breast for about fifteen minutes before you nurse to increase milk flow. Massage may help too. Sometimes starting with the unaffected breast will start your milk flowing and make for a less painful nursing session on the other side. Ask a lactation consultant for help if you are worried that baby's latching on or positioning is producing cracked nipples.

deprived moms may feel that way anyway! Pay attention to your entire body and check your breasts regularly for hard or hot spots. (It's good practice for the early detection of breast cancer to be in touch with your body this way.)

Sore nipples can also be an aggravation many women don't want to endure. The initial tenderness should gradually go away. If not, poor latching and positioning are likely to blame. The baby is probably not getting enough of the areola into his or her mouth. If it hurts, start again. Ask your doctor or

"I had 'overactive letdown' and was told I could have nursed multiples. My baby choked because the milk came down so fast, and she couldn't stay latched for long periods of time. I saw a lactation consultant and even tried the 'Australian hold,' which involved holding my infant on my knee while trying to have her nurse from afar. We had a rough few weeks. Cabbage leaves ended up being my savior! When cleaned and cooled in a Ziploc in the fridge and then placed in my bra, they naturally absorb the milk and ease the pain."

Elizabeth

hospital lactation consultant for help if this is a persistent problem.

Here's the thing. *Each of these breast-feeding challenges is very manageable.* You just have to step away from the problem long enough to ask for help and get perspective. Perspective can be hard to come by your first year of parenting—and with each successive child you will likely still be stymied by the crisis of the week. Attitude is everything. If you can endure the ups and downs of breast-feeding, you will give your child a priceless gift, you could lose weight more quickly, you'll save money, and the bonding is worth the bumps.

## The Breast Pump

The breast pump can be an amazing bridge between you and your baby, keeping your nutrition close even when you can't be. When you've established a nursing rhythm, introducing a bottle of pumped milk can put one of those night feedings into your husband's hands. It can also allow *you* the flexibility of the occasional bottle when you find yourself in a place where it's tough to nurse. I could always participate in or even lead a meeting if I was bottle feeding rather than nursing. Pumping can help you continue breast-feeding if you go back to work. Pumping milk to leave behind can also

95

allow you to leave the house without feeling like a cow stealing away from the barn.

Speaking of cows, I had no choice but to pump while my preemie son put on enough ounces to be ready for the real thing. I pumped ten times a day early on and every three hours for the forty-six days before he came home from the hospital, and then at home until he had enough energy for all feedings from me. I had thoughts of renaming myself Bessie. It got old. But faithful pumping really does work to increase your milk supply, and you can see the evidence in ounces!

Don't mess around—buy a high-quality pump or rent a hospital-grade machine to get going. Having a picture of your sweet infant nearby when you pump can help stimulate your letdown. There were plenty of moments it felt surreal to pump milk from my breasts. You might not imagine there are other women doing what you're doing. Then one day you'll talk to someone on the phone and recognize the familiar whir of a pump in the background and you'll smile. You will also smile when you have a child old enough to imitate you pumping or commentate races on which side will "win."

## A Few Hints

Speaking of sides, I don't know many women who haven't experienced very different milk production from her two breasts. I tried with each kid not to favor nursing on the right, but I did and was a little lopsided as a result. Never

"There was a part of me that was really immature because women would just whip it out to feed and I would feel so uncomfortable. Didn't they care that people could see their chest and that they were doing it in public? I had a hard time making eye contact while they were feeding. Now I don't even think twice about it and it's so not a big deal."

Lisa

fear, you return to normal eventually. For women who leak on one side while nursing on the other, quality pads to slip in your bra are a must. Many women I spoke with said they tried all brands and came back to the ones with an adhesive strip to connect the pad and your bra and prevent the strays I mentioned earlier. Washable pads are certainly comfortable but never seemed as absorbent to me and quickly smelled. I don't mention products by name lightly, but Lilypadz are a fairly revolutionary addition to the marketplace that could save you time and trouble. They are breathable silicone breast pads that really function more as a second skin. You can wear them swimming or with an evening dress, as they stay put while inhibiting leakage. Many times in mothering, women will struggle with a product or an issue, only to find out later that someone has already invented just the thing to make life a little smoother. Don't suffer! Explore!

Who imagines that when she has a baby she'll spend the next year sleeping in a bra? Yuck. It's hard enough to feel like your day is now a wakeful twenty-four-hour cycle of feedings. When I get in bed I want to feel "free," not as though I were too tired to undress. But every time I tried to go braless, I'd regret it and create more laundry. The best compromise was a nursing tank top—or any tank with a nice shelf in it. Adhesive breast pads usually stay put, and you can feel together without feeling strapped in. There's also an Australian-made nighttime tank called the Booby Bib, which is like pajamas and breast pads all in one. If the rave reviews are accurate, the sixty-dollar price tag might be worth it.

Whether you wear one at night or not, good bras are a must. Many women try cheapies and go through them quickly. It wasn't until my third child that I invested in something that didn't look like a sterile straitjacket (think 1950s insane asylum). Again, nice things were out there; I just didn't realize it. Amazing what a pretty nursing bra will do for one's self-image at such an emotionally precarious time. Just remember not to put any bras in the dryer. It hastens their demise.

## The Rules of Engagement

As we consider nursing and undergarments, a few thoughts on the rules of engagement. Try to be discreet when nursing in public. It can be done. Often my first son looked like he'd spent an hour in a sauna when he emerged from under a blanket. He spent a decent part of his infancy looking sweaty, disheveled, and bewildered, though full. By my second child I learned that, yes, a baby blanket is great for privacy, as the baby gets latched on, but those smaller square silky blankies, usually more for baby's comfort than keeping him warm, are a lighter drape over a baby's head and his dinner. I'm talking about the ones I thought were a cute but impractical gift and looked more like a doll-size blanket. Two of my children used these blankies for years for nighttime comfort. Practical indeed!

I have nursed everywhere from church to a fancy Valentine dinner in Washington, DC. I did not sit around with my shirt unbuttoned. No one saw my breasts. My kids didn't slurp loudly like puppies at a puddle. I was not out to make a statement. I was just trying to feed my kids what the American Academy of Pediatrics says is best, as well as having a life in the meantime.

Kelly, a registered nurse and lactation consultant, told me she never nursed her first child in public. "I was afraid of being indiscreet. Everything I did, I timed around when he needed to eat—I wouldn't even feed him *at* the doctor appointments

"My good friend told me that she couldn't believe that I wasn't going to be breast-feeding my daughter. She said I was going to have big issues with her getting sick all the time because breast-fed babies don't get sick and bottle-fed babies do. It hurt my feelings, and I held on to that resentment for a year. My daughter actually didn't get sick until she was thirteen months old."

Lisa

but before," she said. "I was very uptight about it all. It was something I didn't think about beforehand and should have." And this is someone very used to body parts and babies and moms nursing in front of her! Kelly said a couple things changed her attitude. She began noticing other nursing moms in public. She had a second child and had to loosen up. And she even discovered something called a "Hooter Hider," a hip and lightweight cover with an adjustable strap that goes around mom's neck with a rigid collar for peering in and seeing what baby is up to.

"With the second child I just had to be more flexible," she said. "I was so much more relaxed and had so much more freedom. I wish I had discovered that with my first child."

Seeking solitude as you are trying to get the hang of nursing is not only normal, it's best. You want to stay relaxed as you are trying to establish your baby's feeding. As I was finding my rhythm with little Zach, my sister-in-law came to visit. She wanted to go shopping one day. I have long admired many things about Lori's parenting, so I trusted that if she thought "getting out" was doable, it probably was. I can still remember finding a mall bench, and then a department store lounge, and then a dressing room, and feeding my baby through the day. I expected that every eye in the mall would be on me, but the truth was that most people never even knew I was nursing a child. It was perhaps the finest baby gift anyone gave me: the knowledge that my breasts and my baby and I were not confined to the house. It opened up our whole world. Actually I think it helped me develop a can-do, even adventurous attitude with my kids as to what was possible for us as a team.

When Kelly visits new moms in the hospital, she suggests they nurse in front of a mirror, to see what other people see when they watch. What an awesome idea for increasing your confidence!

When a baby starts to kick and look around while nursing, usually at about seven months, you *will* need privacy. A baby's sudden distractibility can make you think she isn't interested in you or your milk. In truth, she is just waking up to the

> ## If You Decide to Bottle Feed Exclusively . . .
> - Wear a well-fitted support bra.
> - Place an ice pack under each armpit to help decrease swelling and pain.
> - Take pain medicine as prescribed.
> - Avoid running hot water over your breasts.
> - Avoid frequent touching or handling of your breasts.
> - Engorgement usually goes away in a few days. There are no safe medicines to "dry up" the milk.
>
> Similac Welcome Addition Club and moms who have been there

sights and sounds of the world, and all the stimulation—TV, siblings, you opening mail over her head—can make it hard for her to focus. At that point, intentionally seeking quiet and stillness might be a good idea.

I should say here that to the last day of nursing, my husband was concerned with propriety. I think he always imagined that the baby would throw a leg up, blankets would fly, and a boob would be on public display to the gasps of hundreds of onlookers. As my comfort level grew with each month and each child, so did his. He learned to request a booth when we were out to eat or let me have the window seat on a plane. He learned to tug the privacy blanket back over my shoulder when it started to droop without me having to say a word.

Your husband's support of breast-feeding is important. Occasionally he can be *too* supportive. As one friend told me, her husband's pressure to nurse at all costs led to an ultimate "It's my body!" argument between them. But more often, a man can feel set aside as his new child *requires* mom every three hours. Attitude is everything for both of you. Watch how you ask for things—water, a footstool, that extra pillow—while you nurse. Don't be demanding, just encouraging. Let dad burp, change, and swaddle the baby—and be sure to compliment his technique. Lots of moms say that when dad brings a hungry baby to them at night, it is a huge help, and the child feels daddy's secure arms "rescuing" him from hunger. When dad uses a bottle of pumped milk for that middle-of-the-night feeding, he is wonderfully appreciated by all! My husband loved the excuse to cuddle the baby *and* catch up on a little taped TV. For me it took a little effort to *let* dad help. It was hard for me to realize that I wasn't the only one who could care for our new boys. It's easy, when you are finding your way, to hide your own insecurities under the guise of "I must do it all." Think about it.

Please don't judge another mom's decision to nurse or to bottle feed, not even in the deepest part of your heart or mind. Whatever her reasons—maybe medical necessity—each mother has to decide for herself. As you probably know by now, motherhood is highly personal. But it is also a sorority of hope and fear and heart-wrenching desire to do the job "right," whatever that is. You do a disservice to this sisterhood any time you elevate your own choices over someone else's. Children inspire enough guilt on their own without moms dispensing it to each other. Understanding instead of judging the choices your contemporaries make is not only nice, it's smart. A good mom gathers information from a range of sources, sorts through it, and then does what's best for her own family.

## YOUR BODY AFTER BABY

*Babying Me*

1. What are my feelings about breast-feeding?
2. If I am breast-feeding, what do I like about it? What am I having trouble with?
3. If I have chosen to bottle feed, am I comfortable with my decision?
4. What words describe my body and how I feel about it?
5. What unanswered questions do I have about the way my body is recovering from delivery?
6. Whom have I asked for help or advice? Where might I find answers or relief?

# 12

# Coming Out of the Closet

## *Weight and Clothes*

After you have a baby, your closet is like a boxing ring. On one side hang those tents and T-shirts you're sick of and those pants with a pouch you don't feel you should wear or should need to wear, even though they might be all that fits. On the other side hang pre-baby fashion, favorite shirts that just don't look right over the balloons that are your breasts, and jeans . . . ah, the old jeans. In the middle is you, bouncing from side to side, perhaps throwing a couple of air punches in frustration. There's no clear winner, and your self-esteem can be quickly knocked out.

### How to Cope

When we have so little control—over our bodies, our baby's sleep, our emotions—a relatively small thing, like not being able to wear what we want, can often put women over the edge. Be patient. Be gentle with yourself. Remember how you thought nine months would last forever, and then *boom*, it was over? Same with your weight and wardrobe. If you try on the same clothes every day in hopes that pounds were lost in the night, you are setting yourself up for failure and frustration. This is true too if you do a daily weigh-in.

One friend rids her closet of all the things she can't wear post-baby and puts them in the closet of a spare room. One day a month she lets herself try on her old favorites.

When I had little A.J. two months early, I had to go home without him. One of the first things I did was take the two seasons of bought and borrowed maternity clothes and make a pile of them on my closet floor. When my sister asked what she could do to help, I answered, "Get a tub." For me, putting away the maternity clothes was a very important step in completing something, controlling something, and finding order in something during those early days after he was born. I survived in drawstring pants and the very biggest of my old stuff—often left unbuttoned.

Nursing moms have the special challenge of wearing clothes that fit and are flattering but that can be pulled up or aside at a moment's notice to free a breast. I can't tell you how many times I put something on only to realize I'd have to practically get naked to feed a baby. And oh, the sweaters! They seem a good, comfy choice, but they can turn both you and your baby into a sweaty mess when you nurse. After a

"Having to continue to wear maternity clothes contributed to an ugly, grungy feeling I had in the months right after baby. I felt like a sack of unwanted flesh. It surprised me that every part of my body was affected by pregnancy. I couldn't believe how much weight stuck around months later. But I was equally surprised at how my body repaired itself when I gave it care and priority. After a year I was nearly back to my pre-baby weight."

Lisa

while, choosing the appropriate thing to wear will become second nature.

Most men will never so quickly gain and lose as much weight as moms do. It's hard for them to understand many things about the postpartum mind and body, especially the pouch—the dunlop (as in, when you're done it lops over)—the muffin top. How yummy. Men call their extra middle "love handles," and they rarely come with the emotional baggage of giving birth. Accept that when you go on closet tirades, your husband will try to be helpful or remain silent. You might find his silence frustrating, his words empty, and his assurances about your body ridiculous. He means well, and in my experience, he means what he says. So don't take your fashion frustration out on your husband.

And don't take it out on your checking account. Quickly buying new clothes to fit your new—and temporary—body isn't usually a good idea. If this is your first baby, you have no idea what the first year holds for your weight and waist-line. And you don't want to end up with a bunch of too-big things you bought on impulse. As you will one day tell your children, make good choices. That's not to say treating your-self to a little something new and lasting—new underwear was always my favorite—won't give your self-esteem a little boost. A fashionable warm-up suit in cooler weather is a sound choice, and some new shoes may be a necessity, not just a treat. (See "Meet Your New Feet" on page 109.) One friend told me that, after six months in maternity clothes, the thought of continuing to wear them got her so depressed that she finally broke down and bought some bigger things,

"Clothes will never fit the same. I weigh now what I weighed pre-babies, but I have plenty of clothes that don't fit around the waist. My husband just said, 'Doesn't everyone have a pouch? Don't you just move on?'"

Angela

"I remember getting ready for a football game after having my daughter, and as time went on, I was so aware of my fat hanging over my pants, that I just had an all-out temper tantrum. I actually hit my fists on the ground and yelled, 'I am so gross!' It was good to let it out. I got some perspective. My weight defined my self-esteem. It shouldn't but it did, and realizing that was good for me."

Jenn

and then cut off the tags so the size wasn't staring at her. She kept working off the weight, but having some new things to wear was important to her self-image.

You have to decide what's best and most motivating for you. But remember that the body you have after giving birth is not the body you will have a year later.

## Losing the Weight

Of course the big question is, how long will it take for these pounds and inches to go away? You have water weight, breast weight, and body fat to deal with. Water goes first, and breast weight will likely take months. And yes, some women never get back to exactly the way they were.

Sylvia Brown, author of *The Post-Pregnancy Handbook*, says that skinny moms who gained thirty to thirty-five pounds lose most of their pregnancy weight in the first three months. Borderline overweight, older moms, or third- or fourth-time moms who gain between thirty-five and seventy-five pounds lose most of their weight between the third and sixth month. Overweight moms will lose most of their excess weight six to nine months after childbirth. (From an interview with Brown on Storknet.com, http://www.stork net.com/guests/postpregnancyhandbook.htm.) I repeat these numbers only to reinforce that every woman is different, and it takes everyone time to lose weight.

## Creative Camouflage

**What to Wear**

- Low-on-the-hip fashions (not crack-revealing teenage wear) are very forgiving to a mushy middle. But wear them with long shirts that cover you completely. Pants that come to the waist will make your tummy feel squeezed in like a section of a balloon animal.
- Bigger breasts are often better off with a modest V-neck than a crew-neck style of shirt. A piece of jewelry can be a nice point of interest other than your cleavage.
- Nursing shirts got poor reviews from the women we talked to. They're a great idea, but not usually practical or flattering.
- That said, remember nursing when you dress. Our moms found knits more practical than button-up shirts because of the stretch factor. Many dresses will have to wait.
- Try wearing skirts to feel more feminine and to push yourself out of sweats occasionally.
- Avoid overalls unless you farm. They are too forgiving and will not motivate you to get back in shape.
- Keep the silk shirts in the dry cleaning bag. You are entering an era in your life of unbelievable goo. Spit-up and drool and drops of medicine and leaky breasts all demand washable fabrics.
- Dark colors are slimming. Need we say more?
- If something barely fits in the morning, it won't fit at all later in the day. Be comfortable from the get-go and avoid unnecessary frustration.

"I gained eighty pounds. Eighty pounds! I ate whatever I wanted and thought, I'm a runner. I'll run it off. You hear so much about losing weight breast-feeding. I was down to needing to lose about forty-five pounds, and I was running hard. I felt like I was in someone else's body. I ended up shattering a disc on my spinal cord and having surgery with a four-month-old at home. I did too much, too soon."

Kelly

---

**Mommy Meals:**
**Getting Your Complex Carbs**

**Best Sources:**

- bran
- wheat germ
- barley
- maize
- buckwheat
- cornmeal
- oatmeal

**Good Sources:**

- pasta
- brown rice
- potatoes
- other root vegetables
- peas
- beans
- lentils
- corn
- yams
- oatcakes
- whole grain pita, brown, or bagel breads
- whole grain breakfast cereals, like Shredded Wheat
- high-fiber breakfast cereals, like All-Bran
- old-fashioned oats
- Muesli, without added sugar

---

Your average new mom should take in about 2,000 calories a day. A nursing mom should be eating 2,500 calories—including extra protein—because she burns 750 calories feeding the little one. You won't get the weight-loss effects of breast-feeding until about four months. That's when the level of the appetite- and milk-stimulating hormone prolactin settles down, and your retained fluid has made an exit, but your metabolism is still rocking.

So it's important not to use nursing as an excuse to eat a bag of Oreos in one sitting. If you want to maximize your weight loss, make half your calories complex carbohydrates. Sadly, these are not found in Oreos but in whole grain form, such as whole-grain breads, oats, and brown rice. These break down more slowly and give you a steadier stream of energy

---

"I was asked a few months after the birth of each of my girls, 'When are you due?' That can make you stop wearing tight-fitting clothes for weeks."

Elizabeth

"Isn't it interesting how delivering such a beautiful thing can wreak overall havoc on your body?"

Jennifer

throughout the day. Simple, refined carbs found in processed, convenience foods tend to be devoid of these natural nutrients and are more likely to be converted into fat and stored.

It's a challenging transition to go from eating ice cream at 10 p.m. to wanting to lose weight fast. Most nursing moms I know get surprisingly, intensely hungry as they keep pace with an infant's needs. Prolactin, which stimulates milk production, also stimulates your appetite. Out-and-out dieting is not advised when you are nursing, but this can be a time when you learn to eat healthier. It always seemed my baby and I got hungry at the same time. His appetite always came first because I felt so guilty listening to the crying! And then I learned how to make lunch and nurse simultaneously. (Yes, this did involve mustard on my son's head once or twice—perhaps that's why he has an aversion to it.) One mom I know made herself a sandwich during breakfast to have ready at a moment's notice. It kept her from dragging the Doritos bag to the couch for a quick fix while she fed her daughter.

Check out local fitness classes that you and your baby can take together. Walk to the grocery store with the stroller to get exercise and an errand done at the same time. Do crunches on the floor as your baby (safely) has tummy time on or next to you. I know you are exhausted, but it doesn't get much easier to exercise than in your baby's first sleepy months. And it will help the fog to lift. As baby gets more active, and certainly with successive children, scheduling exercise only gets more challenging.

When someone says, "You're looking great!" they mean it. But you know what baby "souvenirs" you have acquired and may even scoff at the compliment. The same is true when you look at others and marvel that they are back in jeans or seem

## Meet Your New Feet

Stacey's husband knew something was up. They were at a restaurant with their three-month-old.

"Go ahead and go before we leave. I'll wait."

"Wait for what?"

"For you to go to the ladies' room."

"What makes you think—?"

"You look like you're walking on eggshells, like you are about to burst."

She did burst, into a laugh-cry combination he'd gotten used to these last weeks.

"My feet are killing me! I love these shoes! My feet got fat! I don't know why. My life will never be the saaaaaaame!"

It's true. Your feet are also not what they were before baby.

They balloon because of fluid retention, or edema, during pregnancy. We soak them, we prop them, but the pregnancy hormone relaxin is also at work, loosening ligaments in the feet, causing our twenty-six foot bones to spread. It's the same phenomenon that allows baby to enter the world through your loosened pelvis. While we're quite happy for that, the snug shoe phenomenon can surprise us with the discomfort it causes.

Though the swelling abates after baby arrives, any bone spreading is here to stay. And so is the resulting half- or whole-size increase in shoe size. If you can look at the sunny side of things, you get to buy new shoes! But there are likely some old standbys and Friday-night favorites in your closet that you'll try again and again, hoping their tight fit is all in your head until you limp home, pledging to get rid of them. (Your Friday nights will change dramatically too, but we won't go there yet!)

Don't suffer or cause calluses or bunions to form by denying the reality of your foot size. You were probably already guilty of that before you had a baby, right? Give the too-tights to a good friend. And if you plan to have more children, remember, your feet may not be finished growing yet.

unscathed by housing a baby for nine months. From labor to weight loss to child rearing, remember: everyone has their *stuff*, their issues. You might not know what they're dealing with. So don't compare or set yourself up to somehow feel less successful. Take care of your life-producing body, and accept that it is neither what it was nor what it is yet to be.

## YOUR BODY AFTER BABY

*Babying Me*

1. What am I wearing right now? What would I like to be wearing?
2. What have I eaten today? Am I indulging, binging, being smart, eating enough?
3. Do I have a friend or family member I'm able to laugh and talk honestly with about my new body?
4. What's been my past experience with exercise? What are some goals I can set for getting moving with my new baby?

# 13

## Downpour

### *Weathering Your Emotional Storms*

Before I had children, I hosted a few baby showers and attended several others. They were sweet, sugary affairs that oozed cute clothes and small talk. I enjoyed them and soaked up every second of the one thrown for me. Okay, maybe the baby food tasting was over the top, but I felt incredibly loved and special that day. And I simply couldn't wait to meet my son.

Hindsight is, to be honest, a little frustrating. At my shower, no one said anything remotely truthful about those

> "I remember my husband talking about how cool the birth of our son was, what the placenta was like and all these details, and I'm thinking, I hated every bit of it. How come I didn't think it was so wonderful? I felt guilty I didn't love it more. And I wasn't about to share that!"
>
> Kelly

"I always ask friends, 'Have you had your big breakdown yet?' You have to have one, if not more than one."

Elizabeth

first months as a new mom. I had no idea tears would spring to my eyes with only a few seconds' notice after a perfectly fine day. I had no idea the toll of sleep deprivation. I'd been to college—how bad could a few all-nighters be? I'd been in bad moods. They lift, right? I knew motherhood would change my life, but no one told me it would affect just about every decision I'd make every second of every day.

Since then I've attended baby showers and, no, I didn't corner the new mom to say, "Buckle up, babe. You have no idea what's about to hit you." I guess I'm now part of the conspiracy. Every woman deserves those blissful premotherhood days, when buying tiny clothes and deciding what color to paint the nursery are her foremost concerns. She shouldn't try to guess the first time she will dissolve in a puddle of unexplainable tears, any more than she should worry about her unborn baby's first fever. But I can't help thinking that if more women were more open, more forthcoming about the emotional side of having a new baby, maybe we'd all be a little more prepared when it's our turn. That's my hope here, to explore the range of reactions to having a new baby before they take you by storm. It's harder to see the rain, or remember where you keep the umbrella, when it's already pouring on your head.

## The Drizzle

The emotional aftershocks of having a baby start right away—and so does trying to suppress them. No matter how much you think you've prepared, the reality of pushing a human being out of your body, or delivering one by C-section, is

112

overwhelming. This is true even without circumstances like the cord wrapped around baby's neck or your barely making it to the hospital in time.

From the first squeak your baby makes, the focus is now on her. You are left in wide-eyed wonder about what you've just done—delivering your wonderful baby—but the trauma and the pain that you experienced is eye-opening as well. You'd like to talk about these things, but it's pretty personal and you're not sure if anyone is really interested.

You need to find someone who will listen, a sibling or friend who cares and will listen to you. This was your birth day, not just baby's. We recover from trauma by talking about it and releasing it. My dear friend Kristin's exciting labor and delivery happened before her husband made it to the hospital. A friend of hers captured the details of the day and wrote up the story of Jake's birth as a priceless gift. She said it helped her process the process. She passed on that tradition to me, chronicling my youngest's ten-week-early arrival with every detail she was privy to and presenting it to me on his baptism day. She had listened to my ramblings attentively, and helped me make sense of and make plans after his premature birth. Because it was a fuzzy and fast-paced week in the hospital for me, her gift helped all of us hang on to something I might have otherwise eventually lost.

Believe it or not, even awesome memories fade. Whatever your opinion of journaling or your insecurities about how you write, consider taking time to record the details of your

"My son has a scar on the top of his cheek from the scalpel they used to cut me open. That's how fast it had to happen. It was that bad, and they told my husband they weren't sure if I was going to come through or not. My son loves hearing the story of his 'battle wound.' I got a lot closer to God at that moment. I came out of it thinking, I've been given a second chance. And yet it's still hard to talk about."

Stacia

"I picked up toys every time my baby napped. What was I thinking? It's only when you look back you can see it. Especially in that seven o'clock to midnight period, you're so tempted to stay up and get things done. Sometimes, yes, you should watch that TV show with your husband. You need that. But a couple times a week you should go to bed as soon as you can."

Elizabeth

child's arrival. It will be cathartic for you, your child will love to hear the story over and over, and one day it will be a priceless treasure that is passed on, as your kids have kids of their own.

Disappointment is another emotional aspect of life for new mothers that isn't often verbalized. Who on *earth* could be disappointed with a new baby? I'm not talking about go-back-in-you're-not-cute-enough disappointment. I'm referring to letdown, when the expectations of having a baby and the reality don't immediately line up and you feel down. Maybe you had a C-section when you wanted to go natural. Maybe labor happened before you were ready, and you feel a little cheated. Maybe you were a fertility patient and had worked so long at achieving and sustaining a pregnancy that now having the baby instead of *trying* to have one leaves you feeling a little lost. Perhaps it's your last baby, and you had your tubes tied, and there is some grief, or sense of loss, invading your joy. You might also simply miss the feeling of having your child inside you. You are not alone.

There's no "right" way to feel after having a baby. Your mind and your heart were as busy changing as your uterus was during those nine months. Usually these feelings will abate quickly. Talking to your husband, doctor, or friends is key. Sometimes just talking about these "unmentionables" can help clarify what you are feeling and then free you to move on.

## The Clouds

Ever put Windex in the refrigerator or ice cream in the pantry? Ever gone frantically looking for your keys only to find them in your left hand? Sleep deprivation slowly, insidiously clouds your concentration, your decision making, your everything. And it makes you more prone to depression.

It's so subtle. You know you're tired. You know how much sleep you got last night. But you are up, dressed, living life, feeding baby, cooking meals, functioning. You may be having a conversation and suddenly you can't find the next word of your sentence. You criticize yourself for not being more on the ball. You cry when you drop something. You bark at your husband. In the midst of all this, you may not realize that lack of sleep is at the center of the chaos. Sleep-deprived people are prone to mood swings and feelings of inadequacy—as though parenting doesn't give you enough of those on its own!

### Tips for Good Napping

**The Right Length**

A short nap is usually recommended (20–30 minutes) for short-term alertness. This type of nap provides significant benefit for improved alertness and performance without leaving you feeling groggy or interfering with nighttime sleep.

**The Right Environment**

Your surroundings can greatly impact your ability to fall asleep. Make sure that you have a restful place to lie down and that the temperature in the room is comfortable. Try to limit the amount of noise and the extent of the light filtering in. While some studies have shown that just spending time in bed can be beneficial, it is better to try to catch some zzz's.

**The Right Time**

If you take a nap too late in the day, it might affect your nighttime sleep patterns and make it difficult to fall asleep at your regular bedtime. If you try to take it too early in the day, your body may not be ready for more sleep.

Source: National Sleep Foundation

Without enough sleep you can also be irritable and lethargic, crave sweets, and suffer from burning eyes.

When I was expecting and celebrating new babies, I swore I'd hurl the next book that told me to "sleep when baby sleeps." Who was going to pay bills, return phone calls, write thank-yous, make dinner?—you get the picture. Many women, especially those who have left behind careers for motherhood, long to feel productive and high functioning, so they sacrifice sleep for getting that one more thing done. Personally, I also hated being wakened from a nap by a crying baby. I always felt groggy and out of whack for at least an hour after—worse, I reasoned, than if I'd not slept at all. By my third child, I learned how essential naps were and how overrated our personal-need productivity is.

Yes, naps are going to be interrupted, but they are crucial to recovering from ragged nights of disconnected sleep. You can't erase a sleep debt with naps, but you can gradually diminish its effects. For decades researchers have been telling us that children need a good night's sleep to learn. Parenting is the biggest education I've ever tried to attain. It makes sense that we need our sleep too.

The National Sleep Foundation says we need seven to nine hours of sleep for optimal performance. Sleep comes in four phases. The fourth phase is deep sleep, the rich stuff that lets your immune system do its job. Only after the first full sleep cycle is complete do we get to rapid eye movement or REM sleep, when we dream and process the day's stimuli. If you are wakened during any stage of the sleep cycle, it has to start over, so you miss that REM sleep and aren't giving your body the time it needs to adequately rest and your brain the time it needs to properly recharge.

There are logistical issues of sleep deprivation and emotional ones too. The cycle of feeding, diapering, and loving a baby becomes a twenty-four-hour cycle in the blink of an eye. As new parents, you find the day just doesn't stop anymore. You'll be feeding the baby and notice the sun rising, and

## The Yawn of a New Day

### Maximizing Your Sleep

- When your baby dozes off, especially when he's full and freshly bathed, dive into bed. Don't waste time opening mail, unloading the dishwasher, or anything else. Every minute counts.
- Don't watch the clock as you fall asleep. That only increases anxiety and prevents good sleep.
- Watch your caffeine. You may need a jumpstart when you begin to fade during the day, but caffeine stays in your system longer than you think and interferes with the quality of your sleep. When nursing, limit caffeine to one or two eight-ounce servings per day. Caffeine in breast milk reaches its highest level one hour after you consume it and can cause irritability and poor sleep habits in babies.
- Resist the urge to play host to out-of-town guests. They are usually visiting to help, and that means letting you nap.
- Turn off the ringer on your phone when you are going to sleep.
- Turn down the monitor. Baby's breathing and gurgling can keep you alert and anxious when you are trying to recoup sleep. If the baby is in your room, consider napping in a different room.
- When you can, hand baby over to someone else just after a feeding, and then have that person use a bottle at the next feeding so you can spend the entire time sleeping. Longer periods of sleep can make a big difference.
- When you do hear baby, it's fine to wait a few minutes to see if she'll settle back down. You might both go back to sleep if you resist the urge to respond to every whimper. Many times a little fussing precedes settling back down.

you'll long powerlessly to stop it. The day has started—or did it never end?

Several of my friends, as they looked lovingly and bleary-eyed at their new babies, have had others tell them: "You are going to be tired for the rest of your life." At first that seems hopeless and insensitive. But parents of toddlers to teens concur that it's in part true—your sleep patterns change as a parent, whether you are getting little ones a drink in the middle of the night, are up with sick kids, or are waiting on teens to come home. "It's reassuring," one friend told me, "that I'm not doing something wrong. It just is what it is. You sleep less once you have kids." Once you accept that there's a new normal to your sleep patterns, you can go about making the most of what you can get.

The Mayo Clinic and many experienced parents recommend keeping consistent bedtimes for you as well as your baby. Go ahead and get pajamas on, brush your teeth, calm the house in preparation for bed—at a regular time—even though in your mind you might be preparing for a wakeful night with a newborn. Going through the routine will help your internal biological clock, which in turn will help you get the best sleep you can when you do sleep.

I asked my husband what he thought about our sleep deprivation learning curve. He said we just learned how not to stress or take it out on each other as we realized it was a temporary state. He also said, "The first good night of sleep we got after Zach was the night we left the monitor off by mistake." So true. We nicknamed our son "Barnyard" that first year because he sounded like every animal in the farm—awake or asleep. He got through that no-monitor night all by himself. What a concept for a new parent! I'm not endorsing turning your monitor off, but you may want to consider how loud you are keeping it and how instantly you respond to each peep baby makes.

We did learn something else just as inadvertently. When you are trying to sort out the reasons your baby is wailing in the night, you can barely open your eyes, and your husband asks what's wrong with the baby, in most cases he is not saying, "You are an unfit mother. I really want to go back to bed. Can't you figure this out?" Even if that's what you hear. He is simply wanting to help all three of you get back to bed. Marital snapping in the wee hours is normal. It's not pretty, and you should definitely try to refrain, but it's normal. Let it go, and pledge to do better the next night.

As I mentioned, being wakened by crying was hard for me. I find being wakened by *anyone* fairly unpleasant. To avoid feeling as though this were happening several times a night, I tried sleeping on the couch when I first "went to bed" around 9 p.m. That way, when baby woke for the midnight feeding, I felt more like I'd had a good nap than a bad night's sleep. I'd go to my own bed after that, and with one more feeding at 3 a.m., I felt as though I'd just been wakened once. It was a mental game, but I was tired enough to sleep anywhere with my own pillow, and it worked for me.

The couch trick had some other implications too. When I was on the couch, I didn't have to worry about disturbing my husband by turning on the TV. I kept the room dark and the volume low for both baby and me, but focusing on something helped me stay awake. I learned to love catching up on some recorded TV—thank you, digital age—and even sometimes planned to watch something special, so it would be easier not to resent having to be awake. Some women I know did every night feeding in dark silence. When I had the company of the TV, I felt more intentional about middle-of-the-night mealtimes instead of feeding my sons like a reluctant zombie.

Many women have a hard time staying awake in the middle of the night while feeding a baby, and there were times when I'd feed the baby with my eyes at half-mast, hoping to somehow keep the sleep vibe going. Then I'd jerk awake wondering how long I had been dozing, with no idea if the baby had eaten well or fallen asleep himself. Several women I know used a little timer for their night feedings, so if they did doze off, they'd wake up and know how long baby had nursed. I wish I'd thought to try that. Bottle feeding is a little

"I remember being on the phone with my aunt, and I just started bawling. We were talking about nothing—maybe the outfit she sent—and I just had to hand over the phone. It didn't seem normal, but my mom made it seem fine. She knew."

Stacia

different in that babies might gag or take in unnecessary air if you aren't watching carefully. If you are bottle feeding, make sure you have everything ready for a quick nighttime bottle. Why turn on the lights to measure powder at 3 a.m. if you don't have to? Do what works for you, don't hesitate to ask others what's worked for them, and never be afraid to change up your routine if it's *not* working.

My friend Lynette found watching TV during a night feeding frustrating. She was too tired to focus. Also she couldn't find comfort in the overnight quiet of the house. "I remember actually dreading the night coming," she said, "until I finally brought the baby to bed."

Co-sleeping, as it's called, is the source of much debate. Opponents say it's stressful and dangerous. Advocates say it promotes bonding, breast-feeding, and better sleep. It would take more than this entire book to report the full debate and research on the subject. Do your homework on this issue and talk to your pediatrician. I never trusted myself or my husband not to roll over on baby.

Lynette admits she took her baby to bed out of desperation and against what she had read. But as an immobile sleeper, she said it gave her not only the rest she needed but her first experience in using her intuition to do what she felt was best for her family, despite varied advice. Whatever you do at night, do it safely. There are several products that seek to make co-sleeping safer, including side rails—enclosures you

"I don't know why there's such a stigma to taking an antidepressant. It's not like it's tattooed on your forehead. It doesn't mean you are a failure. You just have a chemical imbalance, maybe for a while, maybe forever. I used to say, 'No thanks, I'll be fine.' And my husband finally said, 'You can't do this anymore. It's not good for you or Hanna.' I just know I never want to feel like that again. It's the worst feeling in the world."

Sara

## What to Look For

Any of these symptoms after pregnancy that last longer than two weeks may be signs of postpartum depression:

- Feeling restless or irritable
- Feeling sad, hopeless, and overwhelmed
- Crying a lot
- Having no energy or motivation
- Eating too little or too much
- Sleeping too little or too much
- Having trouble focusing, remembering, or making decisions
- Feeling worthless and guilty
- Lacking interest in the baby
- Losing interest or pleasure in activities
- Withdrawing from friends and family
- Having headaches, chest pains, heart palpitations (the heart beating fast and feeling like it is skipping beats), or hyperventilation (fast and shallow breathing)
- Being afraid you might hurt the baby or yourself

If you're experiencing any of these symptoms over an extended period of time, be sure to consult your physician.

National Women's Health Information Center, U.S. Dept. of Health and Human Services, www.4women.gov

place around the baby directly on your bed—and three-sided bassinettes that attach to the side of an adult bed.

Again, being tired can make you edgy. Consider sleep deprivation a key ingredient to the emotional stew that bubbles about after having a child. But it's important to realize there could be something else cooking.

## The Fog

I think I used to wear sleep deprivation as some twisted badge of courage. Whenever my babies needed me, I was going to be there. But my second son was small, and his little tummy couldn't get him through the night without one or more feedings for months and months and months.

In retrospect I can see that I was increasingly edgy and my patience was disappearing. My husband had been traveling a lot, and I remember standing at the kitchen counter, making some excuse of a meal for dinner, thinking that if my life was a flavor that day it would be sugar-free vanilla. Bland, void, empty. I wondered where the joy had gone. And then I wondered what would cause such an ungrateful thought after the birth of a happy baby. I would talk to friends on the phone but wouldn't really want to be engaged in conversation. And then one such friend asked if I'd talked to my OB lately.

I was still clueless.

Another friend, who had suffered from postpartum depression, saw the signs that I was sinking. I got a little teary on the phone for no reason I could pinpoint. She insisted I pack up the kids and meet her family at McDonald's for dinner within the hour. On arrival, her intuitive husband snatched the baby and a bottle from me. As I watched him smile and ga-ga at my precious boy, I realized something was wrong with me. I adored my kids, but I had lost my own ga-ga.

I called the doctor and welled up just trying to explain why I needed an appointment. By now I knew something was up. When I sat on the exam table, I eyed a purple flier on the wall: the signs of postpartum depression. There I was—my life, hanging on the wall. It had been there for nine months of prenatal appointments, and I'd read it before. And I *still* hadn't recognized what was happening to me. I turned a corner that very moment, knowing finally that I had been living in a fog, and the fog had a name. I was familiar with the term "baby blues," but depression was completely foreign to me. I got down once in a while, but I had to *try* to stay down. I was proud of that. I always bounced back up. I was a floater.

But I'd never been a woman with two kids, a traveling husband, and less than four hours of connected sleep each night for five months. I never realized sleep deprivation exacerbates

---

### Emotions in Motion

**Taking Care of Yourself**

- Get as much rest as you can.
- Try not to spend too much time alone.
- Spend some time alone with your husband.
- Ask for help caring for your baby.
- Keep a diary. Write down your feelings as a way of "letting it all out." Rereading it later will help you see how much better you are.
- Exercise for better sleep and a better self-image.
- Take a shower and get dressed.
- Do something you enjoy every day, out of the house if you can, even for just fifteen minutes.
- Be gentle with yourself. Don't aim for an immaculate house.
- Talk to other mothers about their experiences.

---

postpartum depression. I thought postpartum depression came on quickly after childbirth, not five months later. And I would soon be stunned at how many of my friends—good friends—had been through something similar, and I'd never known.

Perhaps women don't talk about the range and severity of their emotions after having a child because they're not sure what's normal. They are embarrassed—even though postpartum depression can be one of the most common complications of childbearing. You hear of a few high-profile cases but you don't know where your own story fits in. And you try to tell yourself it doesn't.

### The Forecast

Here's what's happening physically. During pregnancy, the hormones estrogen and progesterone increase greatly in a woman's body. After having a baby, these hormones take a rapid dive that researchers think may lead to depression—just as small hormonal fluctuations can change our mood before a menstrual period. There have been studies that support a group of other issues—history of depression, fatigue, marital strife, social support, financial support—as the roots of post-baby depression in women, as well as in men.

The baby blues occur a few days to a few months after giving birth but can make a comeback later in baby's first year due to mom's stress or sleep deprivation. New moms may feel sad, overwhelmed by new responsibilities, irritable, or restless; they may cry often and perhaps have that sense of disappointment we spoke of earlier. Being alone, single, or away from family and the care of nurses can bring on anxiety or fear. The blues, which are thought to affect up to 80 percent of new moms, usually resolve themselves without any treatment within a week or so. Napping when the baby does and reaching out to others can help.

If you've left the work world, for the foreseeable future or a limited maternity leave, this emotional adjustment adds another dimension. Personally, I was incredibly ready to stay home after years of trying to have children, but still I missed the daily interaction with co-workers, feedback on my performance, and having a clear idea of what the day's goals were.

"You lose some of your identity, going from an atmosphere where people know you to being at home changing diapers. It pulls on your heart," Lynda said. "I wish I'd thought more realistically about that before I had my daughter."

Postpartum depression may at first seem like a case of the blues, but it differs in severity. It begins in the first two to three months after childbirth, depletes a mom's pleasure or interest in life, and keeps women from functioning well for longer than a couple weeks as with the blues. It goes deeper than the blues and can feel paralyzing. Estimates vary—and many women are never formally diagnosed—but studies have shown up to 20 percent of moms experience postpartum depression.

"I feel like, after a few years, I can now differentiate between a little fog and a big cloud," says my friend Kelly. "If I felt something, and then felt extreme guilt, it was depression, not just the blues."

Kelly learned the hard way. She was surprised by the instant shift in focus from her to her new son. She had a difficult time nursing and finding help, and she started doubting her ability to be a good mom. Her self-esteem lagging, she started to withdraw.

"I remember sitting in a rocker feeding my son and looking outside at a neighbor mom who had three kids between six and thirteen. They were coming back from a soccer game. I was thinking, *I hate this point in my life. I wish I could fast-forward to that.* And then I wondered what was wrong with me. I cried a lot during the day, home alone, never around my husband. I kept thinking, *I'm not even working; how can I not be happy and have this mom thing under control?*"

For six months she blamed her feelings on being tired. Kelly did start to show her emotions to her husband, bawling as he got ready to leave for work, knowing that she faced another day of "sinking." He'd suggest she call the doctor, and she'd just feel more inadequate and embarrassed. Sharing the warning signs of postpartum depression with your husband

---

### Factors That Contribute to Developing Postpartum Depression

- Having experienced major depression in the past
- A history of hormonal problems, such as PMS
- Difficulty conceiving or repeated pregnancy losses (something that can boost your expectations of parenthood extremely high)
- Delivering your baby prematurely or by C-section
- Giving birth to more than one baby
- Having either a very big or small gap between pregnancies
- Experiencing marital stress
- Feeling isolated or lonely at home
- Lacking family support
- Having experienced the death of a parent during childhood or adolescence

or a family member is important, since they might be more in tune to warning signs you are exhibiting than you are.

Kelly wasn't aware she had something else working against her. She suffered "a little depression" during her first semester in college when her parents divorced. Previous depression is among the factors that make women more susceptible to postpartum woes. Having had postpartum depression also increases the chances you'll have it again. I know with my next child, I was looking for it.

## Clearing Skies

So you think you know what's going on. Now what do you do? See your doctor, soon. One tool to assess your symptoms is the Edinburgh Postnatal Depression Scale, a simple, ten-item questionnaire about what you've experienced in the previous seven days. A simple blood test may also be in order. Sometimes the level of your thyroid hormones is low after childbirth. The thyroid is a gland in your neck that helps regulate how your body uses and stores energy from food, otherwise known as your metabolism. When your thyroid is off, you may get depression symptoms like irritability, fatigue, and difficulty concentrating.

My dear friend Sara had a six-month-old when she started feeling anxious and panicky. "It was like I'd had five hundred cups of espresso," she said. "I didn't want to be alone and I remember having a full-blown panic attack in Hobby Lobby."

A doctor visit found her thyroid was indeed low. But medication, which takes four to six weeks to effect change, didn't take the edge off.

"I thought I was going to crawl out of my skin," she said. "I can vividly remember thinking when I put my daughter to bed, *I'm going to die in my sleep tonight*."

It turned out Sara's thyroid wasn't just low but fluctuating, so medication caused her symptoms to worsen. She was also

> "I cried a lot, and I was tired. I couldn't get a grasp on my life. I wasn't sure of my identity anymore. I felt inadequate immediately after she was born, but it carried over until she was about eight months. My husband came home from work one day, and I was still in my pj's. He said, 'Get dressed. We're going for a walk.' I think joining MOPS (Mothers of Preschoolers) saved my life. It was a reason to get dressed, a place to go, a purpose, a way to serve. I was needed. It wasn't that I was shy. I was just alone."
>
> Lisa

diagnosed with and given medication for postpartum depression. Her experience underscores the importance of following through on doctor visits and blood tests, even though at a given moment, you might think you're feeling better.

Rest, exercise, and good nutrition can help the symptoms of postpartum depression; so can joining a support group or talking to a therapist, psychologist, or social worker.

Another option for many women is taking an antidepressant. It's a step some moms resist because they believe it says, "I can't do motherhood." It's just the opposite. If you had a bad headache that made you miserable and affected your ability to care for your new baby, you'd get help or try something like getting more rest. If that didn't work, you'd take something. You do what is needed to "do" motherhood.

The online postpartum support group says it so well:

Being a mother is one of the hardest jobs anyone can do, and having a mood disorder can make a hard job feel impossible. Many women experience some form of postpartum mood disorders. Having a mental illness is not a measure of your worth, social status, race, or religion. Getting treatment is not a sign of weakness, but a sign of strength and bravery.

Most women can expect to experience an improvement in postpartum symptoms within three months of starting treatment, and the majority will recover within a year. If you are doing well but another new mom you know isn't, don't pull

## The Perfect Storm . . .

My friend Jamie's picture should be next to the word joy in the dictionary. She has an infectious smile and a belly laugh for any situation, especially when it relates to parenting.

Her personality is all the more magnetic when you learn that it was molded through surviving postpartum psychosis, a disorder affecting one or two women in one thousand births.

In her third trimester, Jamie found herself on a sickening roller coaster, laughing uncontrollably and full of passion in the same day that she'd spend four hours crying uncontrollably on her bed. Days of labor, a colicky son, a lack of family support, and a husband with just three days off from work for a new baby combined for "a perfect storm of badness," as Jamie called it.

Jamie's husband, Jason, watched his wife disappear, though her body remained. Without shame she recounts what happened three weeks after having her son: "He cried all day. I cried all day. I wondered who made who cry. I called my husband and told him I wanted to jump out the window and throw the baby out the window too. He rushed home and saw I was sitting by the window, with makeup running down my face. I had actually put makeup on that day because I told myself this was the day I'd stop being sad. This was the day I'd get it together."

Jamie's case of the most severe postpartum mood disorder was textbook, coming on two to three weeks after delivery and bringing with it such symptoms as hallucinations and delusions, illogical thoughts, insomnia, refusing to eat, periods of delirium or mania, suicidal or homicidal thoughts, and extreme feelings of anxiety and agitation.

Jamie was put on major medication and saw a psychiatrist and psychologist weekly, inching her way through her son's first year. Her doctor told her she shouldn't have more children because of her family's history of the illness and the risk of suffering even more severely the next time.

"You can get well again. There's such despair in being that ill, and I wish other women would talk about it. I wholly made the decision not to be embarrassed about it. To have to have your husband learn to trust you again with your own baby—that is embarrassing. But women need to share how hard being a mom can be, whatever they're feeling. You are supposed to love it but sometimes you don't. And you need to find and accept help.

"Motherhood is the most beautiful, painful process there is."

away from her. Be there for her. You may be able to help her find and hold fast to perspective, which is so important. If you can't see the light at the end of the tunnel—and you're in the middle of the tunnel—it's hard to believe the end exists and that you will not always feel like you're in the shadows.

## YOUR BODY AFTER BABY

*Babying Me*

1. Am I getting all the sleep I can? What could help my ability to rest?
2. What has surprised me about my emotions?
3. Do I have a friend or family member I'm able to talk honestly with about my feelings? Am I hiding any feelings from my husband?
4. What are my perceptions of depression?

# 14

## Daddy Dish

### *A New Day for Both of You*

A friend told me the story of her husband going out with friends not long after she'd been through a difficult delivery. He had the chance to relax and have a few beers while his mom was in town to help support his wife and new baby. On his way home, he pulled over to the side of the road and sobbed. He too had experienced a life-changing event and needed a release.

"It made me feel good that he was feeling things so deeply too," she said. "I think I'd been discounting a little what he'd been through."

I know I've never watched anyone—let alone someone I loved enough to marry—endure pain that made him or her scream out. I've never been dressed in scrubs, inches away from where they are doing surgery on my spouse to introduce my new baby to the world. While there is plenty my husband can't grasp about being a mom, there's just as much I can't claim to know about being a dad.

When it comes to understanding your mind and body after having a baby, men can't. After all, we don't fully understand our *own* minds and bodies, right? So while we are enduring so many of the physical and mental repercussions of childbirth, we have to make sure we provide windows for dad to peer through.

I'm not suggesting you alert him to every time you gush blood or have a milk letdown. I said windows, not garage doors. But encourage him to read the post-baby literature from the hospital, especially the C-section recovery recommendations if you've had one. Set aside "couch time" every day, allowing no interruptions, to touch base on how each of you is doing with your new world order. If there is something he *can* do to help, ask him. He cannot read your mind.

Men can find a woman's emotional aftershocks from giving birth particularly hard to deal with. Imagine if *he* were crying at the drop of a hat and all you could see was an innocent little infant at the root of it all. He hasn't lost anything from inside his body. He's gained something—his first tangible look at and feel of the role he assumed nine months ago. And, like you, he's gained a lifelong responsibility overnight.

As the love of my life says, "Even the perfect husband can't help postpartum. You can't fix it and you don't want to make her feel worse by suggesting there's something wrong with her. You're between a rock and a hard place." Todd says that knowing about the reality of the blues and depression was key to not urging me to take a mind-over-matter approach to dealing with it. I wouldn't have taken well to that. So make sure your husband knows the warning signs of postpartum depression. His clear mind can help when yours is on leave.

Stay close to your husband physically and emotionally, even though your mind and body may feel less than lovable. Maintaining intimacy may look different as your body heals and you begin integrating a child into your home, but it's even more important to your marriage now. (Part 3 in this book, *Dealing with Dad*, offers much more on staying connected to your spouse.)

With a new baby at home, resuming your sex life may be the last thing on your mind, or it could be a fairly dominant thought, especially if those last months of pregnancy were uncomfortable and sex was off limits. You may be anxious for a familiar intimacy to balance the many changes in your life. I'll bet your husband is.

Many doctors recommend waiting six weeks before resuming intercourse, though of course some couples do not wait that long. When your bleeding has stopped, any tearing has healed, and your vaginal area is comfortable again, it's usually fine to have sex. The six-week checkup is an ideal time to put your mind at ease and a sensible milestone to work toward. That said, if you are ready sooner, talk to your doctor. You want to avoid additional bleeding or introducing infection, and if you've had a C-section, you must guard against undue stress on the incision.

It's quite likely sex won't feel the same. Think about all that your body has been through. The muscle tone in the vagina could be decreased, and that can decrease your ability to be aroused, at least for a while. Kegel exercises, done by tightening your muscles as if you're trying to stop a stream of urine, can tone your pelvic floor muscles. You may also be dry and tender and should consider a vaginal lubricant to make sex more comfortable. Go slowly, and don't be frustrated if the first time or so isn't your idea of ideal.

*Don't forget birth control.* Many a surprising conception has happened in the months after having a baby, whether the woman was nursing or not. Birth control is definitely something to check in with your doctor about at your six-week visit.

You might be thinking, *How in the world is anyone thinking about sex right after having a baby?* Plenty of women are with you there.

"I felt like a cow," Denise said. "I'd had doctors touching and poking me, and I'm a very modest person. Having that first baby was traumatizing, and for a long time it was uncomfortable having sex. But keeping emotional and physical intimacy is something you need to do. It will fill *your* tank too."

It's extremely important to nurture your marriage physically—whether it's through sex, hugs and kisses, or holding hands. Talk about your needs, where your body is in healing and dealing with your new world. Consider different times of day for intimacy if bedtime becomes a weary blur. Freshen up with a soothing shower and fresh nightie. Feed the baby before you rendezvous to give yourselves plenty of time.

Even though sex may not sound appealing, you might be very glad you went ahead and made love. Or you may talk about some other ways to satisfy either of you sexually if you simply aren't ready for intercourse. Sometimes moms live in their heads, but leading with your heart and body can be very rewarding.

These months after having a baby are indeed like riding a roller coaster. Sometimes you want to grab the hand of the person you're riding with, to scream and laugh together. Other times you want to dump your fear and nerves on your spouse. Be gentle with one another, but do *be* with one another. The ride will even out. And sharing both the thrills and chills, well, that's what makes a family a family.

## YOUR BODY AFTER BABY

### Babying Me

1. How is my husband doing emotionally? Have I asked him?
2. Have I shared my feelings of depression with my husband?
3. What three things can I do to develop emotional intimacy with my husband?
4. Where am I with physical intimacy? Have my husband and I discussed resuming our sex life?

# Happy Mothering

## *Embracing Your New You*

Whether this is your first or fifth baby, the time after a child is born is one of heightened sensitivities and change. There's a new person in your house, and I'm not talking about your baby. You are not the person you were before you brought this little person into the world, but you can emerge from these months a better woman, an undoubtedly stronger one. The best is yet to come.

Happy mothering. Happy babying *you*.

# Part 3

# Dealing with Dad

# Introduction

## Joining Forces

*It was just a few hours. They're fine. He's the dad, after all.*
My husband's first time alone with our newborn was about to end. I'd been to a friend's baby shower, my first outing after having our first son, and I couldn't wait to get home. I felt oddly tied to the little guy, as if I'd been cast out like a fishing bobber to float around in my sleep-deprived state, and the strong bond already established between my son and me was relentlessly reeling me back home.
*He needs me. I think they need me. They must need me. I am the mom, after all, keeper of the milk and all sage decisions about this baby's every moment.*
When I walk in, the house is quiet and a bit messy. They are lying together on a blanket in the living room, exchanging adoring looks. I think I butted in. I think I'm jealous.
It seems my loving husband had taken our six-week-old to the library, gotten him his own library card, and checked out a few books. It was ridiculous and utterly admirable.
"It was so fun to do something that was his first," Todd said. "Everything he does is a first, but it's usually with you."

137

That simple outing was the inaugural run of the adventurous, why-not, could-be-fun, let's-learn-something attitude my husband has brought to every day of parenting since then.

He does things his way, and I think I've finally learned to let him.

Nothing enriches a marriage—or stretches it—like the addition of a child. Mom's fatigue and a crying baby wreak havoc with your sex life. Babies are expensive. Date night requires the help of a third party if you want the date to go anywhere. The household chores are harder to get done, and delegating might be a new concept. Mom and dad each have their own style of parenting, both eager to be successful and appreciated.

A new life also brings daily joy and the opportunity to share it with the person you love most in the world.

Several of the baby books I devoured began by extolling the importance of putting your marriage first. Usually I skimmed that section. *I'm already married*, I thought. That part was "done." I was in search of the how-tos for producing an amazing and manageable child.

Well guess what? All babies are amazing. Manageability is an attitude, not a goal. And the books were right. Loving your mate—giving him top priority—gives your child a secure start in this world. Both of you are learning to dance when neither of you knows the steps. Occasionally you will step on each other's toes. But the tango of trust and the waltz of what-ifs were never so rewarding.

# 15

## Asking for Directions

### *Letting Dad Find His Rhythm*

From the moment my husband began changing our baby's first diaper in the hospital, I knew parenting was going to be an exercise in learning how to keep my mouth shut. He was loud—joyful but loud—as the baby cried, and he went through wipe after wipe after wipe, trying to scrape that tarlike meconium poop off our little boy. He dropped the diaper, and the bassinet started to roll away. It was a hysterical scene that his parents watched, laughing and doing little to help, except hand him those seventeen wipes. I could tell they loved what they were seeing: their son and his son on the first of many adventures. They enjoyed being spectators, but they would be nearby if my husband ever needed them.

It was a great lesson for me, who, had I been able to get out of bed, would have been suggesting, instructing, and generally trying to take over the whole procedure.

Dads have to find their own rhythm and start bonding with baby on their terms. Looking back, I should have been

> "At the end of the day, who cares if the diaper isn't on exactly right? Let the man of the family make his mistakes. I think the most fun comes from making some mistakes and figuring it out. And it's also important from a bonding standpoint. I had Taylor for three days once, and I let him play through one of his naps. He didn't go down for like an eternity. It was crazy. He was so tired he couldn't sleep. I learned that lesson better because I learned it; I wasn't handed it."
>
> Brandon

thrilled that my husband was so excited about changing a diaper instead of worrying about his technique. Some dads aren't comfortable with their miniature, helpless newborn, and they leave the baby stage to mom. What a shame! Even while still in the womb, a baby knows dad's voice and is ready to connect that sound to a strong set of arms and a comforting scent.

When my third son spent seven weeks in the neonatal intensive care unit, the nurses encouraged moms and dads alike to lay their tiny newborn on their bare skin. Those valuable minutes we had with A.J. changed the way I looked at bonding and daddy time. It was limited, and most often Todd and I went separately to cradle that two-pound boy and all his tubes. I was experiencing what most dads do on a daily basis with a healthy newborn at home: a limited window in which to forge a connection with someone you aren't sure knows you are there. Like many dads, in those early weeks, I struggled with the feeling that my baby seemed more like a project than a person.

Moms have to facilitate the connection between dad and baby. We must try to make that window of opportunity bigger, and not stand, nose against the glass, judging his every move.

I know a man with a very loving wife, who has been known to stick her hand out like a crossing guard holding a stop sign when he's attempting to help. It drives that dad batty. Most men are trusted with decisions of great consequence at work, but at home they can be repeatedly second-guessed. Maybe your hand isn't out, but do your words halt your husband's efforts to parent?

My friend Tracy said life with a newborn was far from the ideal picture she had developed in her mind. Her world felt rocked, but her husband's seemed to be business as usual.

"I contributed to that," she said. "I made him feel the baby could do nothing without me. I'd leave them together and come back and say, 'You didn't feed him at three? That's going to mess up my whole day.'

"I'd criticize what outfit he picked, how he fed him, how tight the diaper was. I just wanted to do it right. I wanted everything to run smoothly, and mistakenly I thought he ruined that every time I left."

Tracy's husband eventually let her know she might as well take the baby with her if she was always going to come home frustrated about how he did things. So she finally relaxed, realizing that doing things differently didn't mean doing things wrong.

Mom, decide what really matters. I've never known a dad who didn't at some point pick an outfit for a child that made mom's jaw drop in disbelief. Somehow they can always find the one shirt with the stain or the pants you put in a storage tub because they had become high-waters. But if the child is safe and comfortable, who really cares? If it means that much to you, let your husband know gently without tearing down

> "I remember the day our third daughter was born, my husband brought the other two girls to the hospital in half-pajamas and half-clothes. He thought they went together. They had Fourth of July ribbons in their hair. It was December! It was all wrong. But I thought, Why do I care? They're here and they are happier than they'd be if I dressed them perfectly. I want them to have the greatest relationship with their dad, and to trust him. And they do."
>
> Tania

his efforts. Actually I think my husband enjoys seeing my reactions to the wild wardrobe combinations he picks out—or allows our boys to choose. But finally I've discovered that there are much more important things to worry about than a kid wearing mismatched socks or sleeping in his play clothes.

Some things, of course, are nonnegotiable. If you see your husband feeding popcorn to your eight-month-old, you must say something—hopefully without losing your cool. Maybe tear out that baby magazine article on choking hazards and ask him to take a look. You'd hope for the same caring-not-condemning approach from a friend, wouldn't you?

Sleep, discipline, and safety are the things my husband and I have decided we must approach in the same way. What are your nonnegotiables? Ask yourself, *Is this a one-time daddy-is-doing-it-his-way moment, or is it working against a healthy habit I'm trying to establish*? (We're still debating whether it's a safety issue when dad thinks it's not cold enough for a hat and jacket and mom does.)

Sleep is a biggie, and in our house we say you must "respect the nap." That means when it would be really fun to run by Home Depot, you don't do it if you know your child is ten minutes from naptime—even if she seems pleasant enough at the moment. As you grow as a parent, and your baby hopefully grows into a flexible child, you can decide when to push her and if you can afford the consequences. But early on, respect the nap.

Some dads like to learn things on their own. It's the old resistance to asking-for-directions syndrome. They prefer their one-on-one time with a child to be governed by seren-dipity, and they will resist attempts to program it. That will be hard for you to accept if you are the kind of mom who lays out clothes and a packed diaper bag the night before you make a fifteen-minute trip to the grocery store. But you must let dad be dad.

Some fathers may be eager for you to share that article on bonding or that flier on daddy story time at the library. They want some direction and suggestions but not a three-color PowerPoint on how they should spend time without mommy in the room. Ask your husband how you can help him find his groove as a parent and expand his comfort zone. Ask him to let you know when it's more helpful for you to back off. Don't set him up to fail by watching him drive away, knowing he forgot the baby's bottle. That's just mean—and not good for your baby. He'll meet up with plenty of trial-and-error moments all on his own, just like you will.

Deep in the heart of every parent is an aching desire to do this job well. To hear the words "You're a great mom" is like being handed a glass of lemonade on a scorching summer day. It's refreshing and it keeps you going. I don't know why it's hard to remember that dads need affirmation as well. Maybe it's because they seem so capable and strong in other arenas. We seem to have no problem pointing out what they aren't doing or what they could do differently, but what about the gifts they bring to fathering—those things that make you glad he's their dad?

One friend's first child spit up more than he kept down. She found burping him very frustrating and one night, in a moment of hopelessness, turned him over to her husband. It turned out that he had the magic touch.

"I am so glad I let him try," she said. "Otherwise I would have never known."

Another friend's husband would sit with their baby on his lap and play video games, which really got under her skin. "I finally decided to talk to him about it. I didn't realize he wasn't just playing video games. He was telling him all about

"My husband was recently dusting off a fan, and I didn't even realize I had stopped to watch. Without even turning around my husband said to our son, 'Mommy likes to watch me do things to make sure I do it right.' Ouch!"

Vanessa

143

"I think the biggest mistake couples make is around expectations. We put a lot on our husbands and set the bar very high. One year I decided to let my husband take care of the Christmas stockings. He got the biggest kick out of going to Wal-Mart, but he bought absolute junk. Nothing sugar free. Nothing educational. I was horrified. But the kids played with the stuff in their stockings more than their major presents. He also started the tradition of hiding their stockings. What a hit! I said, 'It's yours, always.' You have to let them parent in a way that's natural to them."

Denise

sports, explaining who his favorite players were and why, and bonding with him in a huge way," she said. "Granted the baby was five months old, but they were bonding. He didn't need to be cooing at him to connect."

My husband swaddled far better than I did, creating perfect little burritos out of his baby boys and their blankets. He is still able to sing a crying child into submission and infuse his boys with a wide-eyed sense of possibility. It began when he held them as babies and told them about famous military battles. He's always been a grand storyteller.

Tell your husband what you treasure about his fathering. Ask him what he thinks his strengths are.

Finally, find humor in each other's missteps, and tuck away memories of your goofs. My mom recalls a day she left us home alone with my dad, and he simply forgot to feed us lunch. Just forgot!

My friend Jenn told me she and her husband were so sleep deprived that one night he put their baby back in bed without a diaper. Kristi remembers her beloved dressing the baby in a snap-up onesie—putting her arms where legs go and her legs where arms go. Write these things down! They are the patches of the quilt that is your parenting. Each square makes you stronger and wiser and contributes to the bigger pattern of love and grace you are trying to create together.

## DEALING WITH DAD

*Looking Inward*

1. What can I do to encourage a strong dad-and-baby bond?
2. How do I feel when my husband does something differently than I would?
3. Am I prone to instructing my husband rather than just letting dad be dad?

# 16

## Riding Shotgun

### *Strapping Yourselves Together*

When relatives are in town, and we outnumber the seat belts in the car, my family occasionally does something we like to call "the double buckle." Two people click themselves together in the same seat belt, usually overlapping each other and often sucking in their collective gut for a short ride. It's not the safest and takes closeness and personal hygiene to a whole new level.

The last time I double-buckled it happened to be with my husband. (Don't worry; he wasn't driving.) Once I remembered that thankfully, yes, I had just brushed my teeth, I got a little thrill from being in his lap. It struck me how long it had been since I'd been there. In college, piling in and cozying up were the norm. As newlyweds and for years after, I'd crawl into his lap spontaneously.

With a new baby, there is quite literally something that comes between a husband and wife. Stick with me here, and move away from thinking about highway safety.

As parents, it's crucial that you double-buckle. You must stay close physically and emotionally and face the bumps as a team. Overlap your hands and your hearts as often as possible. Remember those days of electric proximity and hang on to each other.

In a car you'd never put a baby between you and your husband in one seat belt. They have their own straps and buckles. It's the same in everyday life. You are responsible for your children's well-being, but that doesn't mean they have to be front and center all the time. The primary safeguard of their life is your marriage.

Putting your marriage first might seem automatic and logical to you. It didn't always to me. We tried for years to have kids, and I assumed that when they finally arrived we were to give them our everything. That's what makes you a good parent, right? Protect them at all costs, scrutinize everything from the brand of diapers to their academic development, decide what they should do and when and with whom, read to them daily. My responsibility screamed to me: kids first! What I should have heard is: kids always!

Growing up is a marathon, not a sprint. New parents need to calm the sense of urgency they have about doing everything for their kids—doing everything right and doing it all right now—to see that their long-term strategy for parenting is what matters.

The most important piece of your parenting strategy is maintaining a strong marriage. Harmony between mom and dad injects a household with stability. It nourishes the emotional development of a child. Remember how you felt when your parents argued? Because parents are their kids' world, their arguing colored everything and may have scared you. When our kids' world begins to quake, we can't underestimate the snaking cracks that form in their emotional foundation and stick around long after the quaking has stopped.

Yes, arguing is normal and will likely happen your entire marriage. It can even be healthy for kids to see, depending on how you resolve conflict. But even though it's normal and you resolve conflicts quickly, it still affects your kids, and only you and your spouse know how much quaking there is going on.

Also it's important to keep in mind that it's not just what your children see you do in your marriage that impacts them, but what they *don't* see you do. Do you hold hands? Do you greet each other? Do you forgive? Do you trust? Do you laugh? If you are emotionally blank with one another, they learn from that too.

Kids, of course, make life busier. You've probably already started the routine of "You get the diaper bag, and I'll get the baby." That can develop into "You take him to football practice, and I'll stay home to nap the little guys." Soon you are dividing and conquering every time you go anywhere—out of necessity. I liken it to a football team. Different coaches handle different aspects of different players, but when it's game time, a united front is crucial. Be mindful of staying a husband-wife team whenever you can for the tone it sets for your family.

By integrating children into your life, not plopping them at the top of the family totem pole, you accomplish several things. You are establishing emotional security. You are also modeling marriage and male-female dynamics, and what a huge responsibility that is! Often I think of the parents out there molding my future daughters-in-law. The idea that my little men will love another woman someday is tough to think about! I pray for these little girls to become generous, nurturing women because of what they see in their parents.

"My parents didn't just kiss. My parents made out in front of us. I have to say that felt really awesome. I can remember the feeling it brought to me to know that they were in love. That's really important to who I am today."

Hillary

> "Your marriage is like a beautiful garden. If you don't take care of it, it will grow full of weeds, no matter what great plants you started out with."
>
> Denise

One day all our children will leave the nest. If they leave a nest that has been completely transformed to fit their every whim and wish, they are in for a rude awakening. The world will not cater to them that way. Certainly the comfort and happiness of our kids should be important to us, but there's far more to parenting than "padding" the world for them. I want to raise servant-hearted, appreciative little people, not kids who think the world owes them something.

Another thought: when it's empty nest time, you don't want to be left to share the rest of your life with a stranger. It happens every day to couples who have so focused their lives on their children that they have forgotten the reason they chose their spouse in the first place. It's incumbent on you to stay linked with your partner in a very real way.

## DEALING WITH DAD

*Looking Inward*

1. How are my husband and I setting priorities in our marriage?
2. What gifts does each of us bring to parenting? How are we supporting each other as we find our groove?
3. What's changed most for us as a couple since having a baby? What are our biggest challenges?

# 17

## Table for Two

### Ideas for Staying Connected

We're a goal-oriented society. Meet someone, check. Introduce him to the folks, check. Engagement, check. Marriage, check. Thrive in career, check. Get pregnant, check. Have baby, check, check, check, check, check.

The milestones in our babies' lives are spelled out. They learn to eat, to walk, to talk. Formula and diaper companies send mail on coping with each stage, just as your child approaches it. Then they go to school and are promoted grade after grade after grade.

Marriage is different. This precious, life-giving relationship—one that statistics show has to fight to stay alive—doesn't come with guidelines or graduations. What's the last marital "check" you had? The last time I was told what to do as a married person was when, on my first anniversary, I was supposed to eat frozen wedding cake. No advice has ever come in the mail on keeping marriage from getting stale.

> "We had good jobs, made decent money, and hung out. It was one giant date. We played all the time. How did we not know that was ending? We thought adding a baby would just add to our current life, not create a new one. It's a good life, but it's very, very different."
>
> Liz

It seems easy enough with a newborn. They sleep a lot, and even though parents are tired from the twenty-four-hour cycle of caring for a new life, they have time to catch up and focus on each other. That is, if they can talk about something besides their new addition.

Make no mistake, a newborn baby should be a blessed new center of attention. Every movement is mesmerizing, every feeding a great adventure, and every day holds new things to experience and accomplish. But as baby grows, something starts to happen quietly and gradually—and to the best of parents. Kids get more demanding and more vocal. They require more of your heart, your pantry, and ultimately, your marriage.

When Todd and I were young marrieds living in California, we thought nothing of seeing two movies in the same day, or even driving an hour to Hollywood to see one, just because we could. That's four hours of sitting next to each other, not counting the leisurely lunch and drive time we had in between. The thought boggles my mind as we now have to carve out minutes just to finish sentences to each other. During a rare recent trip to the movies, we actually ate a take-out dinner we snuck into the theater. Time was limited, and, well, we really wanted to see a movie. How's that for staying connected?

*Date night* is certainly one way to stay close. Look forward to those evenings. Leave notes for each other that say, "Can't wait to hold your hand!" Plan *together* what you'll do. Newborns sleep in fairly predictable stints, which makes an ice cream outing with the stroller very doable. If you can leave the baby, a date doesn't have to be long, just an hour

"We went into ourselves a little when we first had Sam. For me it was identity; for my husband it was exhaustion. We communicated, but it wasn't about who we were. We were just trying to figure it out. Now we debrief after the kids are in bed. We have a glass of wine and we talk about everything—friendships, work problems. We're always on the same page because we do it just about every day. If we start debriefing just about the kids, we make ourselves stop and go back to you-and-me."

Angela

for coffee or a walk. The important thing is to regain and retain the habit of focusing on each other.

You don't even have to leave the house. Rent a classic DVD for a buck and eat popcorn. Play poker. Cook a late dinner together and eat under the stars or picnic in the living room. Creativity can be more memorable than cash when it comes to a date. Your goal here is to look into your spouse's eyes and relate. To talk about what's affecting your days and your heart. And to hear the same from him.

*Try getting physical.* For now I'm talking about exercise. Walking or hiking together, swinging the tennis racquet, or swimming at the local recreation center will do your mind, body, and marriage good. Google "date your husband" on the internet and there'll be almost no end to the ideas and

"I was so ready, so excited to become a parent that it became the focus. Now that my kids aren't babies needing constant attention—and they like playing at the neighbor's house as much as ours—I'm starting to look at my main relationship again, and it's not the same as it was before kids. My role as a father is changing, and I'm realizing my marriage has too. We went to Mexico for our tenth anniversary and took the kids because I feel like I never get to see them. In retrospect it would have been much more a relationship builder to go by ourselves. I wonder if I feared not having them there because for so long it hasn't been just us."

Reuben

## Retreat and Renew

### The Marriage Weekend

My sisters and I gave my parents a "marriage enrichment" weekend as a Christmas gift when I was in college. It wasn't so much that they needed relationship help as it was that we thought they deserved the chance to get away.

Quite frankly, it was all the vacation we could afford to give them, but we knew they wouldn't want to spend even that much money on themselves.

That weekend, which was offered through their church, prompted my mom and dad to start a regular date night. They were asked to return to future marriage enrichment weekends as facilitators, and they found they had a passion for working with engaged couples. Today they are employed in family ministry, working daily with couples who are beginning their married life or looking to save it.

You never know what seeds such a retreat will sow.

"Why wouldn't you take the chance to get to know even more the one you love?" my mom says. "Even after forty years there's still room to become closer, find more joy, experience more satisfaction from marriage."

While I have to say running into people who have heard my parents give "the sex talk" at a marriage or engaged couples retreat is a little unnerving, I couldn't be prouder that they make their marriage a priority and have spent years helping to fortify hundreds more.

Attending a marriage weekend doesn't mean your relationship is in trouble, just that you want to nurture it. Many churches require preparation courses for engaged couples, but isn't it funny how once you're "in," it's up to you?

Your local church is the best source for finding local marriage retreats. Also the Weekend to Remember network of marriage conferences can be accessed at familylife.com or 1-800-FL-TODAY (358-6329). Learn about Catholic Worldwide Marriage Encounter weekends at www.wwme.org or 909-863-9963.

inspiration for dates from friends and books. Ask around, or check out *Date Night in a Minivan* by Lorilee Craker. You'll soon come up with your own best idea, just from getting the romantic juices flowing.

*Solve the babysitting problem.* Money is often an issue for a young family, and therefore babysitting can be too. Try swapping children with another couple you trust. They get two or

## On the Road Again

### Life with a Traveling Spouse

Having a husband who travels for work is a fact of life for many women. Thousands of men serve in the military, and they are gone for long chunks of time. That's particularly wearing on a new mom. Not only is her best friend gone, but so is her sleep relief, a second set of arms, and the person she wants most to share baby's milestones. Here are a few ideas on staying connected and easing the separation.

### Before . . .

- Beware of "premature detachment." That's when you know he's going to leave and you withdraw because you think it will make saying good-bye easier. You jump in the foxhole and steel yourself for going solo—but he's still around. If you need to prepare, talk about it. But you don't want to be aloof and cause an argument that will linger in the air as he leaves.
- Put current photos in his briefcase or suitcase. Write baby's size on the back in case he finds a cute souvenir while he's gone.
- Plant his favorite snack for him to find during his trip.

### During . . .

- Talk every day if you can, but realize you might be in different time zones or certainly on different schedules.
- Resist the temptation to replay every detail of your day. Create a box in which you can put notes on the kids' notable accomplishments ("Our baby

three child-free hours, and then you do. You can do this the same day or alternate weekends. Usually, leaving baby with an adult is easier for new parents than hiring a teenager to babysit. With your mind free from concerns for your child and the cost of her care, you are free to listen to and enjoy your mate.

This brings up a good point. Try not to dump on your spouse every baby detail and emotion that have crossed your heart and mind in the past month. On your date allow him time to talk too. Let him share the latest from work. Ask questions.

Engage in an activity or go to a place that will remind you that you are people not just parents.

girl started responding to music today!"), so you can remember to share them when he has time to fully appreciate the news.

- Establish boundaries for both of you when it comes to spending time with co-workers or friends of the opposite sex.
- If travel is the norm for your spouse, look at it as just that—normal. Don't think of travel as something he does to the family, but something he does for the family.
- You are busy, but think what a nice surprise getting a love note would be while he's on the road. Express your appreciation for his daddy efforts.
- Don't shop away the time. Spending money might feel good in the short term, but it could add to your stress in the long run.
- Give yourself something to look forward to while he's gone. Watch a good movie.
- Have a friend over for dessert one night after baby goes to bed. Ask a family member or a friend to help you have a few hours to yourself.

**After . . .**

- Hopefully you've created systems that work while dad's been gone. But don't make him feel like an outsider when he returns. Be especially careful not to criticize his care of the kids when he's getting his feet on the ground again.
- Plan some couple-only time if possible, but expect that he might be torn between spending time with you and the kids.
- Reconnect physically. Don't punish him for being gone by distancing yourself.

*Staying connected won't happen by just wishing it so.* It's also unproductive to whine that your husband isn't planning the fun. You can set the tone. Tell him how important it is to you. Schedule it. Write it down. And have a backup plan if a sitter backs out.

*Also, be flexible about your expectations.* Recently, one Friday morning, my husband told me to pack a bag. I had a mighty full day, and the former me would have been flustered at the lack of notice. But I just went with it, so grateful he recognized the need for us to be just us. We were going to spend the night at a historic downtown hotel—even better, at a discounted rate. We had to adjust our plans several times to get the kids situated with his parents, get dinner without a long wait, and generally get in our heads there was no right or wrong way to spend our time. It was a wonderful twenty hours of just being us.

You cannot expect one evening to erase all stress, restore all sleep, facilitate every conversation, or answer every question. But one evening at a time, reconnecting will help you build a marital foundation that will withstand the pressures and distractions of raising a family.

## DEALING WITH DAD

*Looking Inward*

1. How are my husband and I doing at staying connected as a couple?
2. What appeals to each of us as an activity or opportunity to help us stay close?
3. What are the obstacles to our spending time alone together? Have we really tried to find solutions to them?

# 18

## Wanted

### *Diaper-Changing Mind Reader Able to Function on Little Sleep*

"He doesn't automatically know you are exhausted and moody. You have to tell him."

Elizabeth

It's not that I was keeping score, but there was just something about being awake, alone, feeding that first baby, the exhaustion so deep it was nauseating. I'd walk back into our bedroom with a big sigh, maybe flush the toilet unnecessarily. And I'd surely not go to any trouble to slip back in bed quietly. *Huff, huff, flop, roll, siiiiigh.*

Sometimes my husband heard; sometimes he kept right on sleeping that hard, deep, enviable sleep.

Recently my mother shared with me that she did the same thing with my dad.

## Fighting Fair

- Drop the "gun language," as it's called when you wag your finger like a firearm and point out "you this" or "you that." Stick to "I" statements.
- Avoid personal attacks and name-calling. Remember the tremendous power your tongue has to wound or uplift your spouse.
- Don't lose control. Arguments should never be abusive and should never be so explosive that you aren't able to stay beyond your kids' earshot.
- Don't say, "You always" or "You never." Stick to the issue at hand.
- The longer an argument goes, the uglier it can get. Set a time limit. If you don't know when it's over, you probably don't know what you want to accomplish. Figuring that out first can save a lot of hurt.
- Don't make a mountain out of a molehill. Also, just because you could get mad about something doesn't mean you have to.
- Remember, one of you shouldn't emerge the winner. The relationship should.

"One of my clearest memories is pounding the arms of the rocking chair because I felt so alone," she said. "I was frustrated because he was sleeping and I wasn't. But I didn't know how to tell him."

Forty years later women are still trying to communicate at 3 a.m. without words. When will we learn?

New moms and dads face a very steep learning curve, especially when it comes to expressing themselves. Sleep deprivation makes us edgy and volatile. Uncertainty about what baby needs at a given moment can make us defensive. Hormonal shifts make mom prone to communicating with tears, a language that often baffles dad. Moms and dads can both suffer postpartum blues and even depression. Often in women this means overt sadness, whereas in men it can manifest itself in irritability and hostility. When you're both feeling so much that defies words, feelings may remain unexpressed until they explode.

Communication is crucial between new parents. Every day a mom thinks about a gazillion things and makes about as many decisions. She has a nonstop conversation with herself. But it's easy to forget that hubby isn't privy to all those thoughts. He doesn't know this is the fifth time the baby has started to cry and the fifth time you haven't been sure why. He may see that your hair is in a ponytail, but that doesn't mean he knows you are feeling down and unfeminine because you haven't had the time to shower. He may see a full laundry basket (or two or three), but he may not know how important it is to you to get something finished in a day.

Likewise, when *you* see a well-dressed guy come home from life in the grown-up world, you may not know that he spent the day worried about providing for you and his new child on one income.

Mom goes nonstop each day; most likely she's the primary caretaker and, well, she *is* the mom. It's easy for dad to take for granted that she's doing okay—tired but okay. This is what women do, right? His mom did it, and yours did too. But you are probably facing an incredible learning curve every day with your baby. You have doubts. You still need to be taken care of, but you can't expect your husband to read your mind. Sure it would be nice for him to just *know* when you need a cozy robe, a pep talk, and a giant bowl of mocha almond fudge ice cream. We all want to be understood that way.

Help him.

You have to tell him what's going on, or he won't know what you're thinking. And you need to tell him with careful attention to what you say, when you say it, and the tone of voice you say it with.

My friend Vanessa said that as much as she and her husband planned for their first baby, sleep deprivation and quarreling caught them off guard. "We never really argued before then. Now it was about things that didn't even have to do with baby, like making the bed right. I don't even think we realized it was the lack of sleep making us so edgy until he was about two years old.

"I never agreed with 'don't go to bed angry.' We would have never slept because we were always arguing about something."

"Somewhere in that first year, I longed to be a child again. I wanted someone to put me down for a nap, to anticipate my needs. I wanted to be sick just so someone would care for me."

Noell

You are tired and possibly overwhelmed as a new mom. That's not a permission slip to be ornery, but it is encouragement that you're not alone in letting your tongue slip now and then. Sometimes, as sleep deprivation creates a little paranoia, couples can make their new-baby-era quarreling into something it's not. It's likely, though, that your marriage isn't crumbling, just being reshaped by parenthood.

My husband said that as his patience with our children grew, his patience with me diminished somewhat. Unfor-

## Rocky Road

### When Problems Are the Norm

If you were experiencing difficulty in your marriage before having a baby, those problems might be exacerbated by the new responsibilities a little life brings. How do you know if your marriage needs outside help?

All marriages face challenges and even crises, but persistent hostility, the absence of communication, withdrawal, and real or contemplated infidelity are just some of the signs that your most precious relationship could be in jeopardy.

Consult a professional counselor or a pastor trained in marriage counseling if you're not making progress on your own. Respect the privacy of your relationship—even when it's frustrating you—and avoid sharing details with other family members or friends. *This never means, however, that you should endure abuse.*

"I tried for years to change him. I knew it was wrong. My parents' marriage wasn't like that," Stephanie remembered. "But I didn't know what to do about it. I'd always have to wait and see which of his moods showed up. It wasn't until I worked on me that I could see the truth. It was like a light went on inside me: *God hates divorce, but he also hates you being abused.*"

tunately the same happened for me. I just wish I'd realized what was happening years ago. Some days you muster every ounce of serenity and staying power for the little one, and there's just little left for the one you married. Daily I pray for more patience with my husband and for everyone in my life, including myself.

When you do fire up a feud, agree to revisit disagreements *after* a night's sleep, and you might not even remember what you were arguing about. I know this flies in the face of "don't go to bed angry." I'm not saying go to bed angry; just go to bed. A good night's sleep is often the best medication any couple could ask for. When you do put an issue to rest—and ladies, you know I'm talking to you here—let it truly rest.

Finally, avoid the cheap shots that come from communicating *through* your child: "Well, Daddy really loves football, so

If something about your relationship with your partner scares you and you need to talk, call the National Domestic Violence Hotline (NDVH) at 1-800-799-SAFE (7233).

According to the NDVH, you may be in an emotionally abusive relationship if your partner calls you names, insults you, or continually criticizes you; does not trust you and acts jealous or possessive; tries to isolate you from family or friends; monitors where you go, whom you call, and with whom you spend time; does not want you to work; controls finances or refuses to share money; punishes you by withholding affection; expects you to ask permission; threatens to hurt you, the children, your family, or your pets; or humiliates you in any way.

You may be in a physically abusive relationship if your partner has ever damaged property when angry (thrown objects, punched walls, kicked doors, etc.); pushed, slapped, bitten, kicked, or choked you; abandoned you in a dangerous or unfamiliar place; scared you by driving recklessly; used a weapon to threaten or hurt you; forced you to leave your home, trapped you in your home, or kept you from leaving; prevented you from calling police or seeking medical attention; hurt your children; or used physical force in sexual situations.

Taking care of yourself is more important than it's ever been. You have a child depending on you.

> "During the first six months if not more after your child is born, it's a good rule that what is said past a certain hour—1 or 2 a.m.—is forgotten. I think it's easy to compete for a solution and it's easy to misinterpret each other. It's hard to keep an open mind and take that step back when the going gets a little tough. But you have to know when you've said enough and when to walk away."
>
> Brandon

I'm going to stop what I'm doing to change your diaper so he can keep watching the game, okay?" Sound silly? Harmlessly sarcastic? Maybe, but you never want to involve your children in your disagreements. Start now making that a line not to cross.

## DEALING WITH DAD

### Looking Inward

1. How are my husband and I getting along since the baby was born? What do we attribute this to?
2. When is the best time for us to communicate?
3. In the middle of the night when I'm up with the baby, I feel . . .
4. Something that's been on my heart that I've kept to myself is . . .

# 19

## Lobbying for Hobbies

*Finding Peace in What's His, Mine, and Ours*

My mom was in a Yahtzee group with some other young moms when we were very little. I didn't know until recently that it was so important to her that she kept her dice date one night even though her parents were arriving from out of town.

"It was *my* night," she said. "That's how important it was."

My dad was and still is a huge fishing aficionado. It might as well have been written in their vows that he would love, honor, and cherish a boat and any chance he could get to sit on a quiet lake and reel 'em in. Those weekend tournaments began to look a little different to my mom when she was left home alone with three little girls. She felt just that—left alone.

Hobbies take on a new dimension when maintaining them means leaving your partner with the children. And affording your pastimes now means weighing personal pleasure against the expense of raising a family. Before hobbies become a source of resentment, new parents would be wise to com-

"I think it's hard for a new mom to conceive of keeping up a hobby, and it's hard for her to watch her husband spend time with his. We tend to keep score, noting the number of days or hours 'off' each one has. But you don't get anywhere by giving your spouse a guilt trip. Men get time away because they take it. I think women are waiting for someone to give them permission. You have to communicate what you need. I know the last thing you want is to say it, but men need to hear it."

Brandon

municate and negotiate with each other about the hobbies they love.

Some moms feel conflicted about expressing their personal desires, let alone satisfying them. They feel—and rightly so in some situations—that they should deny themselves for the good of the children. Dads are less circuitous in their thoughts. If they want to go golfing or attend a poker night, they say so.

You raise an eyebrow. You're tired. You imagine hours spent alone with the baby. Those thoughts stir up some guilt. You realize he worked all week, but you did too. You both want the weekend to feel like a weekend, relaxing and fun. But there's a third party to consider now.

We women tend to overanalyze, and sometimes men under-analyze. Whichever way you lean, think compromise. That's different from tallying hour-for-hour who gets to do what. See the opportunity to give your spouse some time as an opportunity to love him better. Don't play games. Tell him if you miss a pastime you used to find fulfilling, or that it's particularly challenging to spend big chunks of time alone with the baby on a Saturday afternoon. Talk about how you can work together on these things *before* they become the subject of an argument.

Remember whom you fell in love with. It's likely that a hobby, or at least how your husband approached his joys in life, was part of what attracted you to him in the first place.

My friend Barb became a mom at forty-one. She was fearful that because she had to wait longer than most for motherhood, her son could become all-consuming—unhealthy for him and for her marriage. When baby was one month old, Barb was intentional about attending a women's retreat.

"I knew I had to do it then to set a precedent," she said. "I had to take the plunge. It surprised some people—I got a look or two—but it went really well. I think sometimes moms aren't sure of what's 'right' so they don't look out for themselves."

Moms and dads need to have their personal niches, but it's also important to find something to share besides the kids. For now, it might be a Friday night movie at home, not mountain biking or seeing Europe. It doesn't matter what you do, as long as you do it together. Parenting can send couples in different directions, and that gets even more intense with multiple kids and their many activities. Invest in sharing things now so that time together is a reflex, not a rare experience.

I don't enjoy running, and my husband wouldn't touch a scrapbook page if you paid him. But while sharing pas-

> "Before kids, we understood that as long as we worked hard, we should be able to enjoy our passions. After kids, I didn't understand why I couldn't still go out in the woods for a week of hunting or fishing without a major guilt trip when I returned. It was my not wanting to own up to my newfound responsibilities as a father, and I took it out on my wife. It got to the point where I dreaded going hunting or fishing because I feared the repercussions when I got back. This made me resentful, and that made things worse. Instead of understanding where she was coming from, all I cared about was how I needed to make myself happy. Ten years of marriage and three kids later, we have learned to compromise regarding my hobbies. I am so thankful for my wife and her understanding of me and of pastimes that are as much a part of me as my hands and feet."
>
> Chris

"Don't begrudge something your spouse is passionate about. Love is letting the other person find him- or herself too."

Mary

sions isn't always possible, sharing what they mean to you is. I understand that pushing himself physically makes my husband a happier guy. It's not about running *away* from us. In the same way, he understands that cropping is a way for me to process where I've been as a mom and that it feeds my need to create, journal, and finish things. I like the outcome of his running. And he likes the outcome of my scrapbooking. So we give each other space and respect for these things whenever we can realistically.

*Realistic* is the operative word. You can't do it all when you have small children. You have to accept that some things will take a backseat for a while. And this may be frustrating. But for me, it would be far more frustrating to want kids and not be able to have them. So, gratefully, I embrace this season and know that likely, in the next, I will be able to do more of the things that give me personal fulfillment.

And I embrace my husband, without trying to hold him hostage from doing the things he enjoys.

## DEALING WITH DAD

*Looking Inward*

1. Before my husband and I had children, what activities inspired us? What did we love about them?
2. Do we "keep score," noting the time each of us spends on personal pursuits away from the family? Are we both getting what we need?
3. What activity could we share during this season of early parenting?

fed

e of Providing

ith my first son, I'd slide
ind caress his little clothes.
iany were things I couldn't
do something for the child
ny unborn son, but I sure

to collect his "stuff." We
continued accumulating.
, but I could get him that
vas sure would be a big hit.
ey back now! I don't re-
how I wish someone had
eeds. I wish I had known
rs—and how much would
i family and friends that

Studies show that money is the number one source of marital strife. Usually that strife is the result of couples leaving their expectations for how they will live and how they will spend unspoken.

"Beginning or expanding a family doesn't bring on new financial issues as much as it amplifies any and all of the financial issues the parents were already facing," said Jordan Jackson, a presenter with the Good $ense ministry. "I would strongly encourage new parents to use the experience of having a child as a great motivator to implement good financial basics. . . . Resist the cultural message that you and your kids deserve to have it all right now."

When developing a financial plan with your spouse, be honest and candid about how each of you grew up viewing money. Then together create a plan for your growing family. Looking at the big picture while baby is still a baby can prevent you from hitting serious bumps later in your marriage.

## Preparing for the Unthinkable

What will happen to your child if something happens to you and your husband? It's a stomach-churning topic but a necessary one. You can draw up a will and have it notarized, or you can consult an attorney to write a will for you. And be sure your loved ones, especially those who will be affected by it, know it exists.

With your husband, answer the following questions when deciding the potential guardianship of your children:

- What are our values in raising our child? What are our thoughts on education and our religious convictions? Who is best suited to follow through on our wishes?
- Who already has a good relationship with our child?
- Where do they live?
- How old and how healthy are they?
- Do they have children? How would the couple's children affect the future of our child?
- How would this couple feel about being named our child's guardian?
- How do finances come into play? Would raising our child be a strain?

> "I don't spend money that I don't have. I don't want money to have power over me."
>
> Vanessa

And don't forget: little eyes and ears will observe your habits and your child will grow up absorbing them.

For new moms who go back to work, the huge cost of child care will be a big issue. When mom stays home, it can be a tricky emotional and practical transition to drop a paycheck and gain a family member when the couple has been living a lifestyle that requires both incomes. A man may grow nervous about being the sole provider for his family. A woman may feel uneasy spending money when she isn't earning any. These are normal feelings. Guilt and worry aren't productive, so if you are experiencing these emotions, stop and think about what is generating them. If you make an effort to spend smarter, your feelings of guilt or worry should go away.

It's hard to refrain from buying your child the world when that's what you want to give him. But a four-month-old has no understanding of ownership. Give him wrapping and ribbons to play with at Christmas. Let grandparents buy a few gifts. Having willpower is so, so hard when you've envisioned your child's first holiday season in full-color daydreams with lots of presents under the tree. Soon enough children understand the concepts of quantity and even quality but not in those first couple of years. Enjoy that while you can. Give experiences. Love extravagantly. Cater to the senses. Those things don't cost much, if anything.

Couples are wise to discuss the holidays long before they arrive—whether you'll travel, what you'll spend, what you hope to be able to say about the season on January 2. Different expectations, often the result of different upbringings, can burst the holiday bubble for new moms and dads and lead to Grinchy arguments. Talk about it.

## Free Gifts to Give Your Child

- Self-esteem
- Faith
- Patriotism
- Literacy
- Attention
- Imagination
- A servant's heart
- Creativity
- Unconditional love
- Time

Then there are birthdays. I still favor going easy on presents out of common sense, being a good steward of your money, and not wanting to create a sense of entitlement in your kids. But I love to celebrate each child's unique role in our family in a big way. We take themes to extremes, but we don't spend much money. For our celebrations we've built a four-car cardboard train and a fourteen-foot space shuttle. I made a fire truck cake with my son pictured in the driver's seat. We've had a treasure-hunting, plank-walking, tattoo-wearing pirate party in which my husband stayed in costumed character for three hours. But we've never spent much on these affairs. We've proven that big fun doesn't have to mean big funds.

Well in advance of the big day, *before* you get swept up celebrating the milestone, decide what baby's birthday is going to mean to your family and for your finances. Then stick to your decisions and stay within the budget you set. It's easy for even a little home party to become overwhelming and expensive.

There are many ways to budget your money, and the women I interviewed offered a range of money-saving tips like buying seven hundred baby wipes at a time and shopping consignment

"If I had stopped and thought about seven years of overlapping college, I wouldn't have bought all the baby things at six months old. Keep life simple. Focus on your marriage. Don't be subject to your peer group. Keep the blinders on. You don't know what's really going on next door, with money or anything else."

Hillary

> ### Looking Down the Road
>
> Here's a great source for objective information about Section 529 college savings plans and other ways to save and pay for college: **www.savingforcollege .com**. There's no investment selling or individual investment advice here but solid information, including a simple college calculator that lets you plug in your child's age and see what type of saving is necessary for higher education.

stores. They extolled the virtues of saving for college and taking kids to the park for free. But hands down the most heartfelt financial advice moms shared was this: beware of peer pressure.

Be clear on why you're buying what you're buying, they said. Don't covet your neighbor's things or feel you have to keep up. Keep your eyes on whom you're parenting, not what they're wearing or what class they might be taking.

Take time with your husband to answer the following questions about your financial goals and your approach to spending.

## DEALING WITH DAD

*Looking Inward*

1. How were my husband and I raised to think about and spend money?
2. What's most important about how we experience the holidays? Are we willing to incur debt to give gifts?
3. What were our best birthdays growing up? What made them so?
4. What should our guidelines be as we approach a big purchase?
5. Are we savers, spenders, or a combination? What would we like to change about our money habits?
6. What is being a stay-at-home mom worth to us? Or what is being a working mom worth to us?
7. What are our educational goals for our children? What will it take to achieve them?

# 21

## Private Time

### *Intimacy after Baby*

The last time I walked into a Victoria's Secret, I ran into six teenage couples passing time in the hot pink store as they waited for a table at a nearby restaurant before homecoming. They were all dressed up, giggling, and straining for some semblance of cool amid the mixed company. All I could think of was my three little boys being young men one day. I wanted to call each of those kids' moms and let her know that her precious baby was laughing at lingerie. Suddenly I felt one hundred years old.

I'd gone there to look for some pajamas, something feminine and fun, yet tasteful, to replace the fuzzy, formless, oatmeal-colored sleepwear my husband had recently told me he couldn't stand. But amid all that silky stuff, all I could think about were those kids, and my kids. Did this mean the honeymoon—on which I'd worn a different nightie every night—was truly over?

"One day you're a fox; the next you have flab dropping over your granny panties. You think I'm ugly. I'm fat. The baby's been pulling on me all day." If there's one thing I could tell new moms it's this: things are not going to be pretty every single day. Marriage is not always a home run, a Super Bowl, a five-carat diamond. But if my husband wants a hug, I stop. I hug. When the kids were little, there were times I thought I was too busy. Don't be too busy. Your marriage is everything."

Hillary

There's no doubt having children changes your sex life. Your body has been through an amazing transformation. If you're breast-feeding, your body may feel like someone else's property. A lack of sleep and an abundance of new experiences may have you feeling anything but your old self, both physically and emotionally.

Your husband may be on a very different page, eager to reconnect with you after this huge life change. But you, though also eager to reconnect, may be self-conscious about your body.

Physically, it is usually safe to resume intercourse six weeks after you deliver, as long as you feel comfortable, any stitches have healed, and your bleeding has stopped. It can take a little longer or less time, depending on the woman and the labor experience. After delivering a baby, vaginal dryness is a common problem but can be remedied with a lubricant. Don't be shy about asking questions or voicing concerns with your obstetrician at your six-week checkup. Discuss your options for contraception if you do not want to become pregnant again right away. It can happen, even when you're nursing.

That's as much as any pregnancy book ever told me about post-baby intimacy. I was looking for a chapter titled: "Am I Ever Going to Feel Like It Again?" Sexual desire is a private concern, but one I've come to learn many moms struggle with.

If your sex life is back on track after having a baby, congratulations and keep on! For many a mom, the months after having a baby give new meaning to the word *drained*, and sex is the furthest thing from her mind.

In general, women are more emotional than men, and men are more sexual. If anything, having a child makes a woman *more* prone to needing that emotional connection with her husband before she feels sexual. Flipping back and forth between the roles of wife and mother isn't as easy as flicking a switch. Think of people as engines. A man is often revved with a quick turn of a key, if that. A woman needs to be recharged. To refocus after a day of diapers and drool, you might need the jumper cables of conversation and hand holding to hum for a bit before feeling ready to roll.

Neither way is wrong; it's just the way most men and women are wired. Try not to retreat into yourself or draw away from your husband if you are feeling blah sexually. Discuss with honesty and respect how your urges and impulses have changed, and try to have this discussion before you're doing it in the form of a heated disagreement.

If conceiving was difficult for you, procreating—not pleasure—may have become the focus of your love life. If your pregnancy was difficult or high risk, it may feel like forever since you made love. Celebrate your new child by renewing this bond with your husband. Denise Vezey, author of *Sizzle: Seven Secrets to Reignite Your Marriage*, has advised thousands of young moms to be intentional about remembering that marriage came before motherhood.

"We put our husbands on the back burner emotionally when we have a baby. It's how God wired us, to be protective and nurturing to our kids. Most husbands understand that for a while," she writes. "But it's not just physical intimacy that they miss. They feel left out. They go from being most important to being pretty low on the list.

"I put so much into hugging my babies that I just didn't want my husband to touch me. But just because my cup is full thanks to children doesn't mean his is. That's where women grow up. You realize it's not all about you."

There needs to be a balance between looking out for your own needs and fulfilling his.

So how does mom recapture her sexual rhythm? Here are a few thoughts:

*Be aware of biology.* Some drugs, such as antidepressants, can dull your sex drive. Talk to your doctor if you sense that something more than adjusting to parenthood is going on with your sexual appetite. Feeling lethargic can also be caused by an improper diet. Make sure you are eating enough, getting enough calories, and staying properly hydrated, especially if you are nursing. Coffee and soda don't count!

*Think sexy.* What makes you feel feminine? Does exercise get your heart pumping? Does renting a romantic movie wake up your sensual side? If you want to be in the mood, you need to get in the mood. Take the initiative.

"We text message each other a lot," Tania said. "We keep fun-loving communication going during the day."

If you are full of good intentions but empty of urge and energy at the end of the day, try mornings, or invite your husband home for lunch. If you find yourself wide awake after a 3 a.m. feeding, your husband probably won't mind if you waken him. Talk it over with him. Most likely he'll be eager to figure out the best time for the two of you.

*Care what you wear.* It was a real wake-up call when my husband denounced my fuzzy sleepwear as completely un-attractive. I really didn't think he cared what I wore to bed. But here's the thing: I was the one who didn't care. I wasn't concerned about what he thought. Be the woman you want to be. If you want to be desirable and full of desire, wear something that says so. I'm not talking garter belts and fishnet stockings, just something cute, something you feel attractive in. Your post-baby body doesn't need to be hidden head to toe. I tossed those well-worn oversized pj's away in favor of drawstring pants and a tank top, and it surprised me how much better I felt about myself. I got comfortable again in my own (stretched) skin and with a little more showing. My husband was happy too. Be proud of those curves and what they created! You are your own worst critic. Your husband will likely care more about your loving attitude than your extra pounds.

"My mother never came out in the kitchen without a robe on," Vezey shares. "Finally I know why. She wore see-through nighties every single night. She wasn't even a striking woman, really. Never talked to me about the birds and the bees, and when I got my period I was afraid to tell her. But she never, ever wore something ugly to bed. I think there's something to learn from that."

Lord knows my wardrobe has seen some serious changes since I had a baby. It's easy to get frumpy when those work clothes are just not working for you anymore and you pick an outfit knowing it will likely get baby smudge on it at some point in the day. But somewhere between silk shirts and sweatpants is the hip momma you want to be. Take a little pride in your outside, and your insides will feel it.

*Set a date.* It may sound utterly unromantic, but many women I know put sex on the calendar.

"I remember kind of laughing when it came up in a group of women I was with, but I was intrigued. I thought, *If it works, it works,* so I talked to my husband about it," Vanessa said.

"We look at it as our day. I do little things to help me get mentally in the mood, and I don't feel like we're going straight for the goods anymore, but it makes our sex life a priority. It's a disservice to your marriage if you don't do that."

Vezey sees date setting as a positive step in making her marriage a top priority of her life: "Try to take a nap in the

"It's important to keep your man happy. He needs to make love to you. It's not right or wrong; it just is. It's more simple than we women make it."

Tania

afternoon. Make it a priority that day. Don't just think about having sex, but truly plan your day so that you have energy for it," she said. "Have your husband put the kids to bed, so you can have a bubble bath. He may see that he can help you get in the mood by taking on more responsibility."

*Think out of the box or at least the bedroom.* Motherhood is quite often an exercise in losing control. On the other hand, you have the power to make your husband's day. How's *that* for control? Surprise him. It's quite possible to return to the steamy days before baby, but it just may take more effort than it used to.

One woman I know gave her husband "the look" while her kids were happily playing. Another bought some racy underwear. Still another suggested a closet encounter to her husband, whose jaw dropped open. In each case, each woman said it increased her own libido to invite spontaneity back into her marriage and initiate a rendezvous.

Your personal life is indeed personal. Some women are just much more inhibited sexually. If that's you, take baby steps toward sharing yourself more fully with your husband.

One friend confided: "When our child was three months old, I made a chocolate cake to show my husband how much I appreciated his patience with my not feeling very amorous. I think he was genuinely touched. We sat and ate the whole thing together. It didn't start out to be a romantic evening, but it was very, very memorable. Just thinking outside of myself—which is hard after you have a baby—did more than I ever imagined it could."

*Touch base.* When a woman's arms are quite often full of baby, she can neglect to touch her husband—to grab a shoulder, pat an arm, hold a hand. Stay connected with these small gestures, even when you are too tired or stressed out for much more. Sometimes intimacy can blossom from planting tiny seeds.

*Don't give yourself grades, just grace.* Adjust your idea of the perfect setting. Rose petals, champagne, and an hour's

"We have to talk about our sexual relationship more than we did before. We're like two ships passing in the night ... but each night, my son and I greet my husband when he comes home. We're very intentional about that. Dad worked hard for us, so let's love on him. I think that says 'I still care about you. You're still important to me.' He needs respect even though you have children pulling you in another direction. I think it's something women need to remember."

Barb

free time may need to be replaced on occasion by impromptu and quick. It's not the circumstances surrounding your sex life that matter as much as having one. Again, keep communicating. Neither of you knows what the other is thinking. One partner could be tired, but the other might perceive the lack of interest as his or her own shortcoming.

"Thirty percent of the time that we are together, I'm totally not in the mood," a close friend and mother of two told me. "But it's always, always, a good thing afterwards."

A nursing mom may find sexuality a little conflicting when a little person is often glued to her body. It's a good idea to nurse your baby shortly before you have sex, to keep your comfort level and your available time at a maximum. Before baby, your breasts may have played a role in pleasure, but now they often have a utilitarian purpose. Sometimes the feeling of being owned by baby can extend to a woman's whole body.

"My kids provide a lot of fulfillment for me. I have a yearning for their smell, their touch," Tania said. "When I'm nursing, my body is being used by a baby and I feel complete. I have to remember my husband is not having this experience. He needs me, not just talking but physically. I have to be more intentional about time for him."

Several women told me they reached a nursing-era agreement with their husband that breasts were off limits for him during the months they were nursing. That helped them feel less inhibited—less protective of their bodies—during intimacy. One woman told me she simply couldn't have sex during the months she was nursing, a struggle she confided in no one at the time, and a struggle she regrets.

"It just put up a wall between us for a while," she said.

According to noted relationship researcher Dr. John Gottman, the couples he's interviewed aren't talking much about sex, and they aren't comfortable asking for what they need.

"Guys want a lot more sex than women do after a baby is born. Even three years after a baby, women's sex drive is considerably lower than men's," Gottman told CBS News. "But what the men are saying over and over again is that it's not the quantity of sex they want. They want to feel like their wives desire them. . . . That every now and then she's going to say, 'You look delicious in that blue shirt.'"

As your baby gets older, and perhaps you add to your family, intimacy can become more challenging—and more important. Privacy becomes a factor. Kids take up increasingly more time and energy, and lovemaking may land at different priority levels for a husband and wife. One man told me, "A woman can find an emotional substitute. I can't find a physical substitute."

I surely don't want my husband finding a substitute—in his real life or in his thought life. Divorce rates are frightening. On TV, adultery is entertainment. Pornography is

> "I wonder if women change their view on the intimate part of a relationship when they become moms. If a midlife crisis isn't about a man's self-esteem, it's about that. All of a sudden the biological clock has done what it needed to do, and they don't need sex as much anymore. My 'clock' has nothing to do with having children. If there's no intimacy between a husband and wife, the relationship could be any other. You might as well be roommates. Talking about sex is a tough discussion, but it's one worth having if you love your spouse."
>
> Reuben

"It's not just about the sex. The couple that plays together, stays together. Ask for help if you have to, but make the time to make it happen."

Brandon

big business. It's incumbent on a couple to talk about their needs, physical and otherwise, so they can continue to grow old *together*.

I've been known to slip in at night next to my sleeping husband, hoping he won't wake up and then snuggle up with expectations of having sex. Sometimes my sleep needs to be the priority, and other times I'm just selfish for "me" moments that are rare to find raising three children. But I have to admit that sometimes I am not interested in sex.

When my grandfather passed away, my grandmother stopped going to bed at a reasonable time. She told me it was too hard for her to be there, in their bed, alone. A much younger friend of mine died suddenly, and I think of his wife so often, knowing that she'd give anything for another night's sleep cuddled against him, for another chance to crawl in and wake him up.

We know we don't have a day to waste when it comes to our kids. The same is true of our marriage. If I were to go to sleep tonight, knowing my husband would never lie next to me again, would I rest knowing I had loved him and had honored our marriage as best I could? Would you?

## DEALING WITH DAD

*Looking Inward*

1. Have my husband and I reconnected physically since I had our baby? Have I discussed with my doctor any concerns or discomfort?
2. How has our intimacy changed since we became parents?

3. Is my body image affecting my desire for romance?
4. How is sleep affecting my libido? How can I work through this?
5. What could I share with my spouse that would benefit our private time emotionally and/or physically?

# 22

## Cleanup

### *Making Your House Work*

Recently a friend of mine confided her new definition of foreplay: "My husband unloading the dishwasher and giving the kids a bath."

This can be a turn-on, indeed!

Marital researcher Gottman says his studies show that men who do more housework and child care have better sex lives and happier marriages than others. But thinking about the division of household labor may be a new concept for couples who, at one time, were home so seldom they didn't create much of a mess.

The exhaustion of parenting and procrastinating doing chores can collide overnight. If you're a new stay-at-home mom, you may see housework as falling under your job description. Problem is, it keeps falling. A growing child is a growing responsibility, even without the growing laundry and baby's growing ability to slime a highchair. So if you've

> "I was a martyr. I had stopped working and knew I wasn't going back. I always thought, My husband has to go to work tomorrow, and I don't. So I took on too much."
>
> Elizabeth

set yourself up as flying solo on housework, you may one day crash and burn.

Every couple has to find what works for them. Some men have been raised to believe that housework is women's work. Other couples practice a fifty-fifty split, like my friend whose husband irons his own shirts. Don't decide what your arrangement is by *not* deciding. Talk it over, with a promise that neither of you will get defensive or accusatory. Remember, you're on the same team.

My friend Erika said she felt lots of uncertainty and lacked stay-at-home-mom friends when her daughter was born. No more independence, no more contributing to the family income, and no more split chores.

"I really wanted that knight in shining armor, my husband, to come home and rescue me at the end of each day. But he wasn't always shining and receptive to the chaos he sometimes walked into. It was quite an adjustment, since I had always prided myself on being prepared and on top of things," she said.

Erika joined a Mothers of Preschoolers (MOPS) group and got some great advice and empathy for her struggles. She also woke up to the fact that she'd slipped into self-pity.

"I did have a knight in shining armor, but his job was not to save me. I needed to get up out of the ashes, so to speak, and take some control. There was no housekeeper coming, and I had no parents nearby to babysit. This beautiful baby girl was truly a gift, and my job was to enjoy her and somehow create a new family of three. I had to lower my expectations a little and realize that I was not perfect, nor was my home, nor was this lovely baby. I did not have control over everything, but thankfully God did."

Erika's ideas and philosophies on chores eventually found *her* on stage at MOPS meetings. Here are some of the ideas she shares—and her husband's take on them.

## Cleaning

Lose the martyr attitude and aspirations of perfection. Ask everyone you come in contact with what works to help her manage her home. Take the ideas you like.

For Erika, it was breaking up housework into manageable pieces. One day she cleaned upstairs, one day she cleaned downstairs, one day she did bathrooms, one day she grocery shopped, and one day she prepped meals for the week.

"I had more time with my daughter because I didn't do it all at once," she said. "While she napped, I spent time doing something I wanted to do.

"The most important thing I learned was that my family, not my house, needed me 24-7. When it was quitting time, my husband left his office. So each night at the same time, I stopped too."

John said that picking an ending time for household work alleviated a lot of pressure on both of them. "When Erika split up the chores through the week, it was a huge benefit to our marriage, our family, her sanity, her well-being, her confidence, her energy, and our communication," John said. "We felt more peace."

> "The biggest mistake I made was not asking for more help. My husband's life didn't have a bump in the road. But I wanted to do it all. I thought I could."
>
> Julie

## Groceries

Make a complete list of everything your family consumes regularly. Erika put hers in order of her grocery store aisles. Make copies of the list and hang them on a clipboard inside your cupboard or pantry. Check off the item when you run out, so you're making a grocery list as you go. When you go to the store, follow your list of what you need, and you will be less prone to spontaneous buys.

Also, planning out meals ahead of time can help you avoid expensive last-minute dashes to the store. Try to plan the meals for a week and buy the ingredients you'll need all at once.

"I thought, *Great, it's her system and she'll control it*," John said. "After a few times of not getting what I wanted from the store, I learned I had to participate and add to the list. At first, I didn't like the change. But the system worked great for Erika. If she's happy, then I'm happy."

## Communication

"I talked to my husband and asked, if dinner was ready when he came in the door, would he be willing to take turns cleaning up the dishes and putting the baby to bed?" Erika said. He was.

"Once we talked about it, both of us felt more settled and confident in our roles. We agreed to ask each other for help when we were overwhelmed and to keep the lines of communication open."

They also designated a spot for nonverbal communication—mail, to-do reminders, and so on. He got a small chalkboard and she bought some sticky notes.

"Erika would ask me to fix something or do something. Most of the time I didn't because of my schedule, and then I'd forget about it," John said. "She'd get frustrated that it wasn't done. I'd get frustrated because she'd keep asking when I didn't have time.

> "Don't expect your man to be a woman, to clean like one or to love you like one. Button your lip about how he cleans. If you keep picking on him, he will give up. He'll quit trying. His heart will get hard toward you because he can never make you happy."
>
> Denise

"It was great when I could finally see what I needed to do. If she wrote it on the chalkboard, I would get it done. Maybe not today or even tomorrow, but I would get it done. This gave her comfort, and our communication improved a lot."

At first these message areas replaced nagging. Then they became a place to leave encouragement or loving compliments for one another.

"We felt like a team again," she said.

Many couples say that making their household and marriage work after the addition of a baby means adjusting their expectations. When you've been away from the kids and the house for an evening and return to a sleeping family and the kitchen a mess and damp bath towels on the floor, you have a choice. Should you be happy that everyone is safe and happy, or frustrated the house isn't in order?

"You have to compromise," Tracy said. "When I come home, are my counters wiped off the way I would have done it? No. Are the dishes off the table? Yes. If it's not decently clean, I'm not really getting a break. And yet when you're talking about babies and kids, *clean* starts to mean something different."

"I always try to put what I'm feeling into my husband's terms," she said. "I might find a work comparison or a football analogy. I think you have to talk about it calmly, not on a night where you are huffing around cleaning up."

What does your house look like right now? At what cost? Some women seek order in their homes because much of the rest of life with children resists such consistency.

"I felt like a dog on a chain jerked all the time from one immediate need to another," says a mom of four grown children. "Keeping my physical environment neat was the one thing I had control over. I wish I could have just sat with my husband on the couch, been with my babies more.

"One day I overheard my kids in their room with a friend, and one was saying, 'You can't take the toys out of the closet and play with them or my mom will get upset!' It was a real wake-up call for me. Every strength has a weakness and every weakness has a strength."

My strength used to be weekend projects. Before having kids, my home was basically only lived in from 6 p.m. to 7 a.m. The house didn't get messy, or I wasn't around enough to see the dust. When you're home as a mom, those household projects you've been wanting to get to are in your face daily and seem more pressing. But less time is available to attack them. Some moms say they look forward to the weekends like they used to, but with less fulfillment from them. Funny how baby's schedule doesn't align itself with the big game or the pull of the Sunday paper.

"If Saturday or Sunday resembles a weekday," my friend Elizabeth says, "I'm not happy. I've learned how to make them feel different even though sometimes I'm doing the same things."

Discuss the weekend with your husband before you're in the thick of it. If possible, plan time for each of you to tackle what you need to and also have some downtime. You've been used to a weekend rhythm your entire life. Though baby's needs remain consistent, you can still make Saturdays and Sundays fun. Declare a no-cooking night and order pizza. Implement a Saturday morning family snuggle tradition. Go for donuts after church. Make it a goal to visit a different park each weekend. If you have to do laundry, do it, but fold during the football game. Give yourself a pedicure while watching a movie together.

You can still be on your toes as a parent but off your feet as a couple. Your home and housework will always be there.

## DEALING WITH DAD

*Looking Inward*

1. Have my husband and I discussed divvying up some household tasks?
2. What's the chore each of us likes the most? And the least?
3. Which of Erika's ideas appeals most to us?
4. What makes a great weekend for me? For my spouse?

# Looking Ahead

## Who Do You Want to Be?

When you're knee-deep in diapers and show-and-tell, it's hard to imagine life after little ones. But it will come. Already I have visions of the odd reality it will be for my husband and me to sit down to dinner with only our third son remaining at home. (I don't let myself imagine them *all* gone.) I imagine looking over at Todd to share a knowing smile that says, as we often do now when we gaze at our kids, "Look what we did."

Do you have your own sign language with your husband? The high sign when it's time to leave a party? The lip biting that says to watch your tongue because little ears are listening? Years ago the Billy Crystal movie *City Slickers* became one of our favorites. In that comedy about a trio of suburban men searching for deeper meaning at a dude ranch, the late Jack Palance plays a mysterious cowboy named Curly. As they clop along on horseback, Curly holds up a single finger to convey the meaning of life. Curly kicks the bucket in the movie, but while hilariously saving a herd of cattle, each of the friends finally understands what his "one thing," his passion, really is.

189

---

**Want More?**

Continuing to explore the topic of marriage in the busy years of parenting is a wonderful way to honor your relationship. Here are some reading suggestions for enriching your marriage:

*And Baby Makes Three: The Six-Step Plan for Preserving Marital Intimacy and Rekindling Romance after Baby Arrives* by John M. Gottman and Julie Schwartz Gottman

*Father's First Steps: Twenty-five Things Every New Dad Should Know* by Robert W. Sears, M.D., and James M. Sears, M.D.

*Childproofing Your Marriage: Keeping Your Marriage a Priority during the Parenting Years* by Debbie L. Cherry

*For Women Only: What You Need to Know about the Inner Lives of Men* by Shaunti Feldhahn

*For Men Only: A Straightforward Guide to the Inner Lives of Women* by Shaunti and Jeff Feldhahn

*The Five Love Languages: How to Express Heartfelt Commitment to Your Mate* by Gary Chapman

---

Not long after we saw that movie, my husband made me a birthday card that said "You are my Number One thing." We've held up a finger in quiet commitment ever since and signed notes that way. One year I even gave my husband his own cattle drive trip for Christmas (other years, it was socks).

There are moments when our children have had our hands so full that we didn't have the energy to lift a finger for each other. Once I heard a speaker say that in any challenging situation, you should take a step back and ask yourself, *Who do I want to be? Do I want to be a patient, forgiving mother? A generous friend? An inspiring, loyal partner?*

Marriage certainly qualifies as a challenging situation— and a glorious one. Who do *you* want to be? Make it so. Your kids are watching.

Here's hoping your marriage will long be *your* Number One thing.

# Part Four

# Finding Your Own Mothering Style

# Introduction

*Feeling Comfortable in Your New Role*

My first son never liked to lie flat on his back. Even when he was already asleep, the second I put him down on his back, he'd squirm and fuss and fuss and fuss. But he slept like a rock in the car.

So one night, during those overwhelming first weeks home, in that dark-of-night desperation, we brought the car seat to the cradle. Propped up and strapped in as though he were shuttling to the moon, he conked out.

For five months, his bedtime routine was our secret. I was too anxious and embarrassed to mention it to the pediatrician. I knew it wasn't hurting him, but surely I was doing something wrong. Right?

The bathroom fan was another magic sleep aid. The gentle roar soothed my little boy in seconds and protected his sleep—in the car seat, of course—from our barking dog and ringing phone. Sometimes it would hit me, as I thought of my child sleeping in the bathroom: *my baby sleeps in a place where people pee!*

Many months later, a good friend mentioned that if her baby fell asleep while they were out for a walk, she rolled her jogger stroller right into the house and into the bathroom, and she flipped on the fan to prolong the nap.

*I'm not crazy. I'm not alone.* Hearing her strategy was like getting a verbal hug.

It takes time to find your parenting groove, to gain confidence in what you know about your child—and feel okay asking when you haven't a clue. You do it all over again with each newborn. But your first child sends you through uncharted waters as you contend with the opinions, interest, and expectations of parents, in-laws, and old friends. Advice pours in from all corners.

Being a new mom is like being at the helm of a ship for the first time—through occasionally stormy seas and with many well-meaning first mates trying to tell you their own sea tales as you steer. Unexpected buoys cause you to veer one way or the other. Sifting through what friends say is right, the way your mother did it, or maybe the way you wish she had, can send you reeling. Getting your sea legs takes time, and it takes patience with yourself and others. New parents have to learn what to filter, what to try, and how not to offend others in the process.

It's important to remember that you are this child's mom. You may not have every trick and technique in your arsenal yet, but you have a set of sensitivities and sensibilities that you will build on, or deconstruct. That's the journey of motherhood.

As you venture forth, your circle of friends will shift. Your connection with your parents and in-laws will hopefully mature. Your time for others will change. And who you *want* to have time for, well, that may change too.

Surrounding yourself with love and laughter and steadfast support during the early mothering years is crucial. By sharing this adventure—in all its glory and with all your goofs—you can become a better mom, you can be held accountable for your choices, and you can truly enjoy this wonderful season of life. By going it alone—or with superficial relationships—you are shortchanging yourself and your children.

You are raising a child but also growing a mother's heart, mind, and soul. Welcome to the next chapter in your life story.

# 23

## Rearview Mirror

### What You Bring with You

A woman is a walking, talking scrapbook, a collage of memories, experiences, and probably some tattered edges too. You reflect where you've been and whom you've been there with or without. For two or three or even four decades you've been this work in progress. And now it's your turn to shepherd and shape a new life.

Sounds pretty daunting in the postpartum days, doesn't it, when just getting a diaper secure on that tiny tush is a challenge? It *is* daunting, and taking the time to think about who you are as a mother, and who you want to be, is very important. The busy wind of parenting can sweep away all your goals and good intentions if you haven't anchored them in your heart.

It's easy to dismiss the infant era as one your child won't remember, but it's the perfect time to establish your values and your goals—your game plan. Before you know it, you'll be hearing a little voice that reflects yours. Little feet will be

"Cooking with my children will always be important to me because of how fun I thought it was to be around the kitchen when I was a child. I was the third child, so being trusted with a role, helping create something—even if it was only setting the table—meant a lot. Private time with one parent was really big. Going to work with my dad, working in the garage with him, or going on an early morning fishing trip—those things made our relationship outstanding."

Lisa

padding along behind you. You want the path they follow to be intentionally set.

Recently my three little boys were having a postdinner, prebath boogie party—spastically break-dancing in their underwear and diapers. They were bouncing off each other, laughing as loud as the blaring music. This is a pretty common scene in my household—the dancing, the laughing, and yes, the underwear. Growing up with two fairly docile sisters, I often stop my own dancing to marvel at the mass of mini-manliness before me. But on this particular evening, a different thought stopped me. I wondered, *Is this one of those things they'll always remember about their childhood?*

I sure hope so. Laughter, parents who aren't afraid to shake their own booties in a show of family solidarity, a love of music—yes, I hope so.

What do you treasure from your childhood? A place? A feeling? An experience? How can you put those good memories into play for your own children?

I grew up in a very suburban neighborhood with parents who adored nature. Each Christmas season all five of us squeezed into the front of my dad's work pickup and drove more than an hour to a Christmas tree farm. We'd run around leaving hats or scarves on the trees with potential. My mom's tree preference, always fat and full, usually prevailed. Dad wielded the saw. Some years it was bone-chilling cold. One year my dad got stopped for speeding. We always stopped

"My mom, though she worked all day, consistently followed through with family dinner at the table every night. No matter how hectic her day or how ordinary the meal, at the same time we all prayed and ate. I want that for my family and I'm realizing how very difficult that is nowadays."

Kim

at Dairy Queen for lunch. I can still feel the shoulders of my family in the seat of that truck. Tradition, togetherness—there was no question these would become hallmarks of my parenting.

My grandparents lived in a tiny dollhouse of a home. Most of the rooms were precise and immaculate and not too child-friendly. It was hard to get comfortable. But I was always drawn to the sewing room, which welcomed me with a pegboard wall blanketed with family pictures. My mom and her sisters' black-and-white wedding portraits hung at the top, the rest of the images seeming to fall from the unions they represented.

I loved gazing at that wall. A feeling of security washed over me in that room—it was one I belonged in. Probably as a result, family photographs are my favorite art. I splash my kids' faces everywhere and hope that a sense of belonging and security pervades every square inch of our home, no matter what it looks like or where it is.

We should view parenting as a backpack we fill with the necessities—clothing, food, shelter—but one that comes with hundreds of little pockets in which to tuck the true stuff of survival: unconditional love, generosity, humor. What would you pack for your kids? What was in your parents' backpack that shaped your childhood?

My dad was always a stickler for honesty. And now I find that even a little lie out of my boys makes me crazy. Also, my folks let me find my own way many times, with attempts at hobbies I wasn't suited for and boyfriends that should never have been. Learning the hard way is sometimes the best way. It's a challenge not to hover over our kids, whether toddler or teenager, but I'm grateful that independence was nurtured in my childhood.

There will always be things we wish our parents had done differently. Now that you are a mom, sleep-deprived and full of ache for how much you want to give your little person, you will probably have more empathy for your folks and be more forgiving of the things you hope not to repeat. If becoming a parent hasn't already opened your eyes very wide to the past, it will.

It's more productive to learn from your childhood than rehash it. For example, my parents never talked to me about sex. The week of my wedding I playfully asked my mom if she was going to have "the talk" with me. She blushed and said she thought that if I had any questions, I'd ask. I think it was characteristic of her generation to be reserved, if not silent, about such personal matters. I don't hold it against her, but I do plan to be in my kids' faces with information on the topic.

"My parents expected a lot of me, and I learned to be very responsible and goal oriented. But my mom had me when she was twenty-one and then had my sister fourteen months later. At different points in my life I realized she had us close together because she wanted to 'get it out of the way.' She couldn't wait for us to grow up and be self-sufficient so that she could have her life back. The summer before I went to college, she turned my bedroom into a workout room, and I slept on an air mattress in the living room until I moved out.

I want my kids to know that I enjoy every minute of every stage they are going through. When you are buried in diapers, bottles, tantrums, and housework, sometimes it's hard to make the most of each day and spend quality time with your kids instead of always looking to the future. But in that way I want to be different from my mom."

Terra

"The same year I left home, my brother also moved out to pursue his career, and the reality of both of her children being gone for good sent my mother into a deep, ugly depression. She chose to lash out at me particularly, claiming that my lack of closeness with God was the sole cause of the strain on our relationship. The bond with my mom is still strained. But as a mom now myself, I have a much greater appreciation for what she and my father did right as parents. My goal as a Christian mother is to meet my children right where they are, just like God does with us. It will be hard not to have high expectations for their choices and even harder to watch them make their own journeys in life. But when they fall—I want to be there to welcome them with open arms and a nonjudgmental heart."

Elizabeth

My friend Kris said her mother kept her faith, and many emotions, very private. So Kris is intentional about lying down with her kids at night, reading, talking through the day, and especially sharing with them her reliance on God.

You may have been hurt deeply by the actions or attitudes of a parent, a pattern you've sworn not to repeat. Sometimes you need help to follow through on those intentions.

"It took me nine years to realize that some of the things I was doing as a parent were hurtful, things I'd learned from my mom," one friend said. "I wish I'd considered that earlier, but when you are raised a certain way, you don't know better.

"It was all about control in my house growing up," she said. "For that reason I will never make food an issue. If you don't like dinner, have a yogurt. And if you want to post your art on your bedroom wall, go for it."

There's a possibility that becoming a parent could unearth some sadness in you stemming from your childhood experiences, or it could reopen the wounds of grief from losing a parent. Consider talking with a counselor if these feelings are weighing heavily on you. Your baby needs the best of you. Taking good care of yourself emotionally, physically, and spiritually is a great example to start setting.

# FINDING YOUR MOTHERING STYLE

*Taking Stock*

1. What do I hope to instill in my children that is a reflection of my own childhood?
2. What does my husband bring to our kids from the way he was raised?
3. What do we hope to do differently than our parents did?

# 24

## It's All Relative

### Dealing with the Grandparents

It was cold. I was exhausted, and I was with my mother-in-law, my out-of-town sister-in-law, and my newborn son, attempting a shopping outing. My brand-new stroller would not open. I had no idea what I was doing. We fiddled. We banged. Inadvertently we scratched the heck out of the stroller tray on the asphalt, creating permanent scars that remind me of the first time I felt inept as a mom in front of my mother-in-law.

It was certainly not the last time. During the writing of this book, I found myself in tears when, out of the blue, my son, a preschooler, decided he didn't want to go to school. He ran away from me through the building and took a swat at me when I tried to retrieve him. For twenty minutes I tried to regain a sense of calm for us both, trying to figure out what to do and what lesson this experience would teach. My in-laws, one of whom works at the school, both arrived during my breakdown. Within five minutes my son was sauntering off to class—with them.

> "When I think of the relationship between a kid and a grandpar-
> ent, I think there's nothing out there quite like it. It's unique. It's a
> beautiful thing. And yet an in-law relationship—with these same
> people—can be one of great struggle."
>
> Noell

I was mortified and humbled—and many other things. Luckily I adore my in-laws. They are loving, faithful, fun people who give without hesitation. Later that day I was able to tell them how lame I felt as a mom that morning, how empty of answers. I didn't mention that after fourteen years of being married to their son, I still seek their approval. Heck, I still seek my own parents' approval.

Having children changes the shape of your relationship with your parents and your in-laws. Hopefully it will deepen those bonds and enrich them through the shared joy of watching a child grow up. But bumps along the way are normal.

Opinionated grandmas, the unspoken dynamics of grand-parent child care, and their indulgent gift-giving practices can all cause a rift in your relationship. As a new mom you have a great opportunity to prevent problems in these areas by talking them through early on.

When a mom or mother-in-law offers advice—maybe the way she fed or napped her kids—it's likely she's just trying to help. Even if she is indeed *trying* to make you feel inferior, you should still handle it the same way—with respect and a thick skin.

"You've certainly been there."
"I appreciate your perspective."
"I'm just trying to get my bearings."
"I'll definitely think about that."
"I sure am doing the best I can."
"I guess we're always learning."

> "As a grandmother of seven and a mentor mom to a Mothers of Preschoolers group, I have seen that you can really hamper a relationship with your mother-in-law by not being open and honest. I know it's easier for a mother and daughter to communicate—in many cases at least. But if you start out the right way, honest and respectful, it will do wonders. Also, if you go into any relationship with low self-esteem or insecurities—as a mother-in-law, daughter-in-law, mother, or daughter— you're not going to be on the same page. You have to think about who you are and what's behind your feelings."
>
> Jeanine

There are two things at work here: your intense desire to do things right and her desire to be useful in her grandchild's life. If you can break out of *your* role for a minute, it's easier to appreciate hers. I have a friend, a mom of four kids under ten years old, who says she spends a lot of time thinking about her future grandchildren. She's trying to raise her kids to raise *them*, so she strives for gentleness and accountability. She's trying to raise *herself* to be a grandma who doesn't have any regrets about the way she parented, so she doesn't bring along any baggage. It's an admirable, forward-thinking perspective.

It's important to remember these are evolving relationships with your baby's grandmas. Their connection with your kids will grow as your kids do. If something feels off, you can likely change it if you are honest and gentle. That's especially true with grandparents who live close enough to babysit.

"My mom is almost a daily part of my kids' lives. However, she has had to understand that they are ultimately *my* kids, and although she is free to give advice, I won't always take it," Sheridan said. "I also have to be considerate of my parents and not expect them to be built-in babysitters. My mom will watch them whenever I ask, but I try to have other sitters so that my kids never become a burden to her."

Once I saw a sign that said, "What happens at Nana's stays at Nana's." As a new mom, I was insulted by that message.

*This is my precious baby—nine months of work and worry before he even got here! You can't change my strategy when I'm just starting the game!* How far I have come! I still hold fast to my ideals but can let go of unnecessary, or imagined, power struggles.

Starting out, you have to decide what really matters. For example, I don't think an occasional donut is going to hurt my child's diet as much as it's going to help create memories with a grandparent. But I have several friends who are livid when their kids are fed junk by their grandfolks. Your call. All moms have their nonnegotiables, and they should. If my parents or in-laws can't stick to my preferred bedtime, I really have to ask myself, what's the cost this time? If we have big plans the next day, I say so in advance and try to provide every head start I can to help them have a smooth evening together. If bedtime was rough or a child decided not to eat, it's not the end of the world. I'm just grateful for the break, and we might try a different strategy next time. Having a friendly conversation about these things *before* you leave a child in a grandparent's care can go a long way in creating peaceful child-care transitions for all of you. Hopefully over time your children will come to understand that they get indulged and loved in different ways in different places.

"I have learned to give specific instructions on what I'd like done," Elizabeth said. "It was important to explain to my mom and mother-in-law that some things have changed, like laying baby on his back versus stomach, from when we were babies. I even gave my mom a pamphlet from the hospital."

Kim said one painful evening actually paved the way for good communication with her in-laws. Here's what happened at a restaurant when they were celebrating a birthday with extended family:

"My husband, Matt, and I had been struggling with our son sitting in a high chair while we were eating dinner. He would much rather get out and roam from person to person or climb in a lap. We had been fighting this for a while and had just

"I always say to my mom, 'Guess I need to keep having babies if I want to get you here more often,' because I know she'll come for a newborn. I grew up with grandparents nearly across the street, and I always imagined my mom would visit all the time. I just want her to see all the cute little everyday things my kids are doing, to really know them. My mother-in-law lives five hours away, and recently she was here and let my husband and me go Christmas shopping. She spent two hours in my daughter's room, just talking. My daughter showed her every necklace, every treasure. I want my own mom to experience that."

Cristal

recently made a strong effort to be consistent. A short time after we sat down, Colby decided he wanted up. Matt's dad offered his lap, at which point we told him we really needed Colby to stay in his chair. Matt's mother began to get upset because we were not getting him out. After what felt like forever to me with an unhappy, crying child, I looked over to see Matt's dad putting his hands out, gesturing 'Come to me. I'll hold you.' Down a few more chairs Matt's mom is beginning to cry because our son is being forced to stay in his chair.

"At that point, I'd had enough. I stood up and said, 'We're leaving now.' Dinner was just arriving. I am lucky that my husband was wise enough to wait until we were outside to question what I was doing. Shortly after we got home, my in-laws called. I dreaded getting on the phone, but I had to let them know I didn't appreciate their doing things to encourage our child to behave in a way that conflicted with what we were trying to teach him. I said if they couldn't support us, then they would have to spend less time with our son.

"I am not a confrontational person, but this was one area I felt strongly needed to be addressed before it grew worse. There were a lot of hurt feelings and tears that night, but as difficult as it was, there were no gray areas left. After that happened, out of the three brothers in my husband's family, we had the easiest relationship with his parents. We didn't get questioned about our parenting but instead were asked about how they should handle situations to be in line with our wishes."

Each family is different, but I hope you're hearing that it's important to think about and nurture this relationship as you go—not wait for an explosion of frustration. My friend Kelly said her mother-in-law seemed overbearing at first. She was a stickler for a Sunday dinner tradition, one that Kelly liked until the exhaustion of parenting made her feel a little resentful for not having a choice on Sunday evenings.

"She loves her son and she loves her grandson, so I had to just pull the positives out. I don't have to cook, and we live near grandparents—grandparents who want to be with us," Kelly said. "So even though I'd rather get my son to bed on time, or go to bed myself, I had to say to myself, *This is not a bad thing.*"

Some moms face a different issue—grandparents who prefer to love their grandchildren from a distance and not as frequent babysitters. This can come as a shock if you always assumed your mom or your husband's would be the one to help so you could get a haircut or do lunch with a friend once in a while. You may have even thought your out-of-state parents would be more frequent visitors.

The media image of silver-haired, retired grandparents, who seem not to have a care in the world, is far from my reality. Many of my parents' generation need to keep working and can't retire yet. My own out-of-state parents continue to work in a field they love, and my sisters and I and our kids are not the center of their universe every day. I get that. I respect it. And I swap ideas with other moms on how they bridge the gap creatively between grandparent visits.

Try sliding family pictures into an inexpensive photo album for your kids to play with. Make recognizing names and faces into a game. You can even buy alphabet stickers (P for Papa, for example) to combine love *and* learning. Keep pictures of special people on the refrigerator too.

> "My kids have certain activities they do with each grandparent that are unique and special to that relationship. They play cards with Grammy Doreen and Legos with Grandma Donna. I think it's important they have something of their own with each person. They feel important and loved. It's an anchor for the relationship."
>
> Sheri

With some cell phone plans, long-distance calling is much more reasonable than when we were kids. I like to call my folks when one of my boys has done something particularly cute.

## What a Trip

**Traveling with Baby**

Perhaps there is nowhere your parenting is more under the microscope than when you are seated with two hundred other people on an airplane, with nowhere to escape, nowhere but a cramped seat where you can feed and console a child. It takes a village to raise a child, but if your child is screaming from his ears popping, the village can be all around you and yet feel very far away.

Here are some ideas aimed at peaceful journeys.

**Take extra clothes for both of you in a carry-on.** You never know how a flight or the excitement of a trip will affect your child's tummy.

**Don't take up luggage space with diapers.** Take what you need to get there and buy more at your destination. Always keep a diaper, wipes, and hand sanitizer within reach so you don't have to lug a bag down a slim airplane aisle.

**Feed your child on takeoff and landing**, or have her pacifier handy. Swallowing helps relieve ear pressure.

**Though children can travel on your lap free until age two,** consider reserving a seat for your child for long trips, especially if he is busy and mobile. Having him strapped in a car seat on the plane might make for a smoother flight. Ask your airline's policy on half-price tickets for infants or on using an available empty seat.

207

When they were babies, I'd give a call after a checkup at the pediatrician, and now I let my kids dial and say hello, even if their attention span on the phone is only thirty seconds long. Making grandparents part of a regular day, not just a holiday novelty, is important. My parents try to do the same, calling to report to my boys if my dad caught a particularly big fish or to see if my kids are ready to watch an important football game.

If you can afford it, consider giving even modest airline gift certificates for birthday or Christmas presents. You could attach them to a finger painting or handprint, with the caption "Can't wait to hold your hand."

**However long you think it will take you to get somewhere**, allow for more time. Being in a stressed-out hurry will make you forget things, and your children pick up on your angst.

**Take off your kids' shoes.** Kicking the seat in front of them is less appealing without the thump.

**For children old enough to appreciate it, have a few surprises**—toys or snacks—in their bag to be opened only in flight. Once I was advised to take a box of Band-Aids along because children will focus forever on opening Band-Aids and sticking them places.

**For babies, think discovery.** Bring items that can entertain but that can be lost or discarded without worry—Dixie cups to stack, unstack, and put things in; an old cell phone; a mirrored compact for peek-a-boo.

**Always keep a few Ziploc bags handy** for separating dirty diapers, icky clothes, a clean pacifier, etc.

**Keep smiling.** Breathe deeply. Again, your child picks up on your anxiety. Assess the flight attendants early. If you need help, tag the one who made eye contact with or goo-gooed at your child. He or she may have the empathy you need.

**Relax and remember, the flight will end**, and you probably won't see your fellow passengers ever again!

**Explore your airline's website for more information on flying with children.** The Federal Aviation Administration offers a printable "Childproof Your Flight" brochure on air safety for little ones. And the site flyingwithkids.com offers extensive and specific advice on just that.

Homemade gifts aren't everyone's cup of tea, but I like the idea of keeping my kids focused on family, on giving, and on creativity. During one visit to my parents' home, my kids were fascinated by a huge bushel of pecans. They played with those nuts for days in every way imaginable. I pocketed about twenty of them. Later I glued them into a shadow box in the shape of a cross, and my oldest son wrote the letters "L-o-v-e y-o-u" on the rest of them and mailed this gift to my parents. The memory of my little nuts' visit will now live on a little longer.

When a grandparent sends your child a gift, always send a prompt thank-you. Involve the kids. We all know how it feels to experience gratitude, and it's a great etiquette lesson to start early with your children.

My children's Nana and Papa started a tradition twenty years ago of recording themselves reading a book and then sending the book and the tape to a grandchild. My nephew would hear their voices and try to tear apart the tape in an attempt to get to them. My oldest son took his afternoon nap for nearly a year by holding a Thomas the Train book as their voices lulled him to sleep. So priceless! I loved hearing their voices in *his* bedroom.

So often when a family visits grandparents, the newness and energy create an atmosphere that is anything but calm— for kids or their parents. As one friend said, "Visiting relatives is just a volcano. Eruptions of family dynamics happen all the time." If it's mom's parents being visited, mom might revert to her behaviors as a daughter, wanting to please, seeking approval. If it's dad's parents, he might do the same, or turn over some parenting responsibility to the open arms of his mom, to the potential dismay of his wife, who could feel she's working overtime trying to parent under the watchful eye of others with more experience.

When you stay under one roof with relatives, your roles of parent, child, and spouse all compete for your attention—and patience. A new mother—or any mother—can feel particularly stressed by the desire to prove herself a good mom.

"You have your self-esteem caught up in your kids' behavior, right or wrong," Kristi said.

Before having kids, visiting family was a vacation for me. When I had kids, I expected the same—a fun change in the routine. But I struggled every time. There were more hands—I had more help—and yet I'd feel unsettled, sometimes unfulfilled at trip's end. And I was prone to bickering with my husband. Eventually I sorted out the feelings I was having. While my husband was able to rest easy with the help of others, I still felt I was working full-time at parenting, which is the way I should have felt; I'm the mom! So my ache for a break collided with my sense of responsibility. And I wanted extended family to think the best of me as a mom, not to think I was handing off my children.

As one friend puts it, "Once I realized going to my in-laws wasn't a vacation, but an extension of what I do at home, I was a lot happier."

Do you crave time at the end of the day when no one needs anything or expects anything of you? On family trips that time dissipates. You have to ask for time alone, for help where you need it. Just remember to take a step back and get perspective, which can be hard to do under someone else's roof but helps you deal with the frustrations.

"I don't think my mother-in-law ever forgave me for taking away her son and then taking him west," Noell said. "It never fails that the day before we leave her house, she picks a fight, maybe so it won't hurt so much to say good-bye. We recognize that now, we expect tension that day, and we accept who she is."

Partnering with your husband is important as you navigate new parental waters. Just as we are to help nurture grandparent-grandchild relationships, a man should encourage a healthy relationship between his wife and his parents, not "play Switzerland" as one friend says of her husband's desire to stay neutral. That said, asking your husband to take sides can be a dangerous thing to do. Strive together to develop respect for the relatives, honesty, and a team approach.

Jamie, who has what she calls a "prickly" relationship with her in-laws, says when she visits them, she always has a close friend on call back home with whom she can vent or process things, so she's not always complaining to her husband. She's called only twice, but she said knowing she has someone "in her corner"—and someone who will offer honest feedback—helps her remember to put a healthy grandparent-grandchild relationship first and get over her own frustrations.

"You accept a lot. You show love a lot. And you take things with a grain of salt," she said.

A final thought on grandparents. Your mother and mother-in-law are two different people. Don't compare them. Don't wish one were more like the other, visited more like the other, gifted more like the other, or loved more like the other. You'd never want them comparing daughters-in-law, would you? Appreciate these women just as they are, as you would have them do for you.

## FINDING YOUR MOTHERING STYLE

### Taking Stock

1. What do I value about my mother and my mother-in-law? What are some concrete ways that I make these women feel their importance in our lives?
2. When family gets involved, what areas of parenting am I most sensitive about? What do my parents or my in-laws do that I don't like? What are my motives behind wanting to control these aspects of family participation?
3. What dynamics are at work when we travel to see our families? How can we improve on our time spent under their roof?

# 25

## A Discerning Ear

### *Hearing Your Inner Momma*

Perfectionism is the enemy of creation, as extreme self-solitude is the enemy of well-being.

John Updike

I'm not sure how much this Pulitzer Prize–winning writer knows about motherhood, but there aren't truer words spoken about the challenges facing a new mom trying to find her way. We all want to do this job so well, and though the ultimate responsibility for our child lies with us, we can't do it alone.

Advice flows from all directions the moment you announce you are pregnant. It never really stops. One day you too will find yourself offering solutions to problems you haven't been asked to solve. We're all eager to put our hard-earned mommy wisdom to good use.

"My mother-in-law told me a great remedy for an ear infection is to blow smoke from a cigarette into the baby's ear. This was not a piece of advice I chose to follow. After taking my son to the ER for croup, she said she didn't think I should give him the prescribed medicines because of the side effects and that humidity would help the most. I wanted to scream, 'I've had him in a steamy bathroom for the last five days!' Instead I said, 'Oh, okay.' (I went with the doctor's advice.) You pick your battles. Some things are not worth arguing about."

Terra

For now, others are likely the teachers, and you are the student. Each day your insights, your intuition, and your knowledge grow—if you listen to others as well as yourself.

When Kelly's son was three months old, he was sleeping in her bed at night. Her mother-in-law was disapproving and direct: "He's going to bring home a girlfriend one day and still be sleeping in your room," she pronounced.

A weary Kelly took a breath. She told her mother-in-law it was the only thing that had worked to keep the baby from crying all night. She agreed it was a habit in need of breaking. Then Kelly said four very important words: "I don't know how."

That evening, Grandma told her son to take his tired wife out for ice cream. As they were enjoying a treat, the truth came out. Grandma was putting the baby to bed in his crib.

"I think the decision to stay at home or go back to work was the most controversial one I encountered. The opinions were everywhere. I was working full-time when I adopted Daniel, and I knew that I would want to be home with him full-time. I think moms who stay home have a lot of bad information about moms who work and vice versa. Women have to make the choice that is right for them. I can't know what is guiding others' decisions, just as they can't know what guides mine."

Dana

After that night the infant never returned to mom's bed. "It's hard to admit you need help," Kelly said. "He cried again, but I knew I could work it out because he'd slept in his crib. That was huge."

You might feel a little overwhelmed as a new mom. Have you read all the books on child care but are still unsure of yourself? Does conflicting advice confuse you? That's all a normal part of finding your way.

There are certain truths that you can rely on. For example, if you are dealing with a medical issue, perhaps a fever that worries you, always consult your pediatrician. Even if a dozen moms tell you that your baby's fever doesn't meet the threshold for a doctor visit, even if you see similar advice in a trustworthy book like the American Academy of Pediatrics' *Caring for Your Baby and Young Child: Birth to Age Five*, if you are concerned, call the doctor. Often a nurse on the phone can help you sort out whether a visit is necessary. But trust your gut. Someday you will likely be one of those moms who is comfortable monitoring an unexplained fever at home, but for now you are learning.

There's a difference between getting advice from other moms and being judged by them. Advice is well-meaning. When you receive opinions and suggestions, how do you feel? Receptive, threatened, overwhelmed, thankful, annoyed, competitive? Assess your reaction. Try to figure out why you

> "When children are young and you are a new mom, you think that your child should be doing exactly what every other child is doing. But the development of children early on is so varied. I still have to remember that just because my children are not doing something—or are doing more than other children their age—it doesn't mean they are less smart or smarter than others. It just means they are as unique as God planned them to be. His plan is greater than the timing of when they learn to sit, walk, talk, jump, or read. He is in charge, not me."
>
> Tracy

## Couldn't Live without It

Some tools of the trade moms call indispensable—and wish they'd found sooner.

**A sound machine**: It produces noises—like rain, wind, or a heartbeat—that soothe baby and muffle other noises around the house. Some are as small as a paperback book—easy to bring along when you travel.

**The heat buddy**: A large, soft, fan-shaped pad you warm in the microwave to bring comfort to engorged breasts and aching muscles.

**Kipiis**: A clip that turns any napkin or paper towel into a bib.

**Gas drops and the leg bicycle**: Baby's tummy bubbles seem to be popped—or at the very least the baby is distracted—by a drop of simethicone on his tongue. Pumping those legs, with baby's bottom raised slightly, can also work out gas cramps.

**Wet wipes**: Keep them in every room of the house and on every row of seats of every vehicle the family owns.

**The SwaddleMe blanket**: Also called a Miracle Blanket, it allows even the most folding-challenged parent to wrap baby into a comforting cocoon.

**A breast pump**: It gives you the ability to nurse and yet share with your husband the wonder of nourishing a newborn.

**Disposable bibs**: These are especially good for travel. They are not environmentally friendly, but finding a crusty bib in your diaper bag is a drag.

**Diaper backpacks**: Men seem more comfortable carrying the goods this way, and backpacks free your arms from a tote bag that often slides off your shoulder.

**The Pack 'n Play**: One mom calls it "a familiar container," which, if you get your child used to it early, can expand your ability to spend time with other people while your baby naps. It's also a great corral for crawlers while you make dinner or tackle a project that demands some focus.

feel that way and you may open your mind a little wider. You should, because the best suggestions you will hear in mothering will come from other moms. So will some of the worst, and the source of both might even be the same person. You'll have to be discerning.

My grandmother, who raised four daughters in an era lacking five-point-harness car seats, breast pumps, and disposable

> "My first playgroup was obsessed with every aspect of parenting, and that was stressful. We compared everything. If my child wasn't similar to others, I would worry. I finally decided to accept and appreciate Jacob's individuality. I enjoyed mothering more. I tried to go with my instincts, trust what felt right, and pray when I didn't know what to do."
>
> Sheri

diapers, gave me a tiny spiral notebook at my baby shower to jot down memories or advice. She wrote on the first page: "Always look in your baby's eyes when you speak to him. It matters." What an awesome insight! She also said, often, that children should be seen and not heard. I respectfully disagree.

Be gracious when other people grandstand. Remember these moms when you start dispensing your own opinions. Certain topics polarize moms: pacifiers, co-sleeping, working mothers, how early to start anything from solid food to preschool. How can you opine on an issue if you don't *consider the child*? Some children need solid food at five months; others can wait till eight months. Every child is different. Use that as your shield against anyone who might otherwise make you feel inferior. We all make parenting mistakes. We all keep striving to do our best. And we all know our own child better than anyone else on earth.

> "The best thing I ever did was to decide what I thought was best using common sense. Then I used my pediatrician as a sounding board and formulated a baseline for what I thought to be best. By not being a 'clean slate,' with nothing but room for others to write on, I was able to have productive, two-sided conversations when talking with other mothers. Suggestions came in the form of casual conversations rather than 'You know what you ought to do' statements. Then I was able to tweak that 'baseline' according to what I liked or didn't from what I'd learned from talking to others."
>
> Kim

One mom tells a story of being swayed from her "inner momma." A friend wanted to do her a favor by picking up her children from a nature class their kids shared. The boys heard the woman's offer and cried, "No, no!"

"She got in my face and said, 'You know you're enabling them, don't you? They will never be able to separate from you when they get to school. They will probably live with you until they are forty.' Somehow she talked me into letting her pick them up."

### 10 Commandments for Mothers in 1918

When baby advice seems overflowing and overwhelming, consider what women nearly one hundred years ago were being told. You'll see that some advice is solid through time, while other words of wisdom don't seem so wise as they age. This is something to remember as you get and give your share of suggestions.

I. Never give drugs other than those prescribed by the doctor to your baby. It may mean his death.
II. Never give Baby a taste of this food and that food until he is well out of babyhood.
III. Always give Baby a bath at the same time every day and be sure that the water is not over 98 degrees and that he is never left for a moment alone.
IV. Never allow anyone to kiss Baby near his mouth or on his hand. You can save him many colds and illnesses.
V. Never put Baby to bed until he has had a good bowel movement.
VI. Keep Baby out of doors at least an hour each clear day, and in mild weather several hours each day.
VII. Give Baby a bed to himself and, if possible, a room to himself.
VIII. Consult your doctor whenever in doubt. A small consultation fee frequently saves a large doctor's bill.
IX. Read everything about babies that you can get; send to the Children's Bureau at Washington for bulletins concerning care of babies; do everything in your power to educate yourself for motherhood.
X. Use your common sense, plenty of soap and water, and an abundance of good medical advice.

"I have found myself in slight verbal altercations with family and friends with regard to disciplining my son. I try very hard now not to discipline anyone's children but my own. It just drives me crazy when other people try to correct or punish my kid, especially without explanation or with an impatient, angry voice. When you as a parent are working on something at home like sharing, manners, or not throwing toys, you want to encourage your child, as well as correct him."

Lisa

Angry with herself for backtracking under pressure, the mom ended up picking up her children anyway, enduring more pointed comments. But walking home on a beautiful day, her clouds of self-doubt began to dissipate.

"Initially, I was angry. But I know my boys. I know they don't have trouble separating," she said. "I have to respect and listen to my kids. I trust their instincts and I need to trust my own maternal instincts. It's hard if you've been raised as a pleaser."

As you raise your child and start to make a multitude of daily choices, be aware that sometimes a one-time decision starts a pattern you aren't expecting. I can't remember how my first son developed the habit of wearing socks on his hands to sleep. He just said he felt safer that way. Cute, right? We even took pictures. When he started wanting the socks to cover his elbows, I wondered briefly if I was aiding an obsessive-compulsive child. It was charming, not harming, though it did go on for the better part of six months.

Some call these things quirks; others say they are props—something a child comes to need to sleep or eat or be content. I have a neighbor whose daughter sleeps with a dozen or so pacifiers—in her hands, on her chest, sprinkled in the crib around her. Another friend had a son who insisted on wearing Batman pajamas at all times—all times—for several months. Endearing? I thought so. Wasn't my child.

But there's another level of props that experienced moms will tell you to beware of, like rocking or nursing your baby to sleep. I'm the first to say having a baby fall asleep in your arms is a beautiful thing. Savor those precious moments. Just be aware that what may seem like a working situation for a week may not feel so good a year later. Introducing a comfort object early on, like a blankie or a musical animal, can be a great signal that it's time to go to bed but still train your child to get to sleep on her own. Just be sure you don't lose that blankie or animal! The point is, trust yourself but resist bad habits.

"My sister-in-law nurses her baby to sleep for every nap, and I just get frustrated because it interrupts and hampers group plans," one mom said. "Everyone agrees the baby is not getting enough healthy sleep, and she complains about her own exhaustion because her daughter never sleeps more than ten minutes. It's hard to know how to help without intruding. You just want the best for the mom and the child."

When you experience parenting success, whether it's an infant's sleep pattern or a toddler's potty training or a third grader's math mastery, it's natural to want to share your insights. Always remember what it's like to be on the receiving end of information. Praise a mom for her efforts. Suggest but don't preach. Keep your sense of humor, and, when you see the opportunity, help another mom keep hers. You may be just the strand of sanity she needs at that moment.

"You want to be so perfect and do all that those books say—and then you want to burn them," Angela said. "I finally

"My daughter was outgrowing her bassinette, but she didn't like the crib at all. My sister-in-law suggested I hang my clothes over the side to see if being able to smell me would comfort her. I used a polka-dotted nightgown one day. It became Hanna's favorite 'blanket.' For a while it was whole, but then we lost it at a restaurant and went back to find it in the parking lot under the tire of a car, so my husband had to rip it out. I cut it into a few pieces at that point so we'd always have another. There aren't many polka dots left on it these days. She's seven now."

Sara

realized what I wanted was excellence not perfection. There is no perfection."

My friend Noell advises new moms: "It took ten years for me to stop relying on other people to give me a report card for how I was doing as a mom. Do yourself a favor—don't wait that long."

## FINDING YOUR MOTHERING STYLE

*Taking Stock*

1. What's been my most memorable mom-moment so far? What emotion did that prompt in me?
2. Do I trust myself as a mom? Why or why not? Are there steps I could take to gain confidence?
3. How am I at taking advice or suggestions on my mothering?
4. What have I already learned that I would pass along to a new mom or mom-to-be?
5. Have my husband and I started anything with our baby that is destined to become a habit? How do we each feel about that?

# 26

## Friends

### *Finding Companionship and Support in Other Mothers*

I recall sitting at my desk at work, pregnant, amazed by my inability to concentrate. I wanted to surf the Web to find out what was happening in my womb at a given week. I would daydream and doodle name possibilities. My belly was the new center of my universe. I felt bathed in a spotlight of newness that no one else seemed to appreciate. I had a co-worker who didn't even realize that I'd gone on maternity leave. She just wasn't in the childbearing phase of her own life and didn't realize that thirty-eight weeks pregnant meant time to deliver.

When our bodies and minds change that much, our relationships do the same. Old friends bump into your new priorities. Some roll with it; some do not.

I had grand visions of returning to my workplace for a visit, my darling little newborn in tow. I expected attention, conversation, congratulations. I got some of that, briefly.

> "It can be tough when your old friends don't understand how a baby can consume your every thought. They are still going out for happy hour. Your happy hour is now a good feeding or long naptime."
>
> Angela

But as I was leaving, I stopped and turned around and was stunned at how the place where my son and I had been standing was now swallowed up by a strategy meeting. It was like I'd never even been there.

"I think it's just you and me, kid," I said to a pair of big blue eyes.

Historically, I have hated endings. Graduations, departures, even Christmas nights have left me feeling incredibly empty. Friendships don't usually stop on a dime, but even their gradual dwindling can make me sad, even if there's something or someone else delightful right around the corner.

Single friends, childless couples, even those trying to have children are in a different place than you are now. With effort and understanding—and common interests—those friendships can stand the test of time and change. Imagine a single woman, yearning to find the man she can share her life with, hearing a new mom go on and on about her baby's long nights. If you were aching for a family of your own, chances are you might not be too empathetic. It's enriching to everyone involved to connect with friends in another phase of life. What great perspective, and a great reminder, that it's not all about you! And if one day your single friends have children, imagine what a knowledgeable support you can be.

I'm convinced true friendship is vital during the early years of motherhood. Your learning curve is enormous, and so too can be your sense of isolation. In the past, school and work provided an automatic pool of people with whom you could connect. Now you're "home alone" but hungry to share the journey with other women.

"I wanted friends so badly when we moved to the mountains. But with no sidewalks, and neighbors in their retirement years, I found out quickly I had to go to the people. For me what fit was the public library's weekly story time. Reading brings moms together. I listened intently and found out more information about my community the first three weeks of attending story time than in any other venue. While I didn't feel comfortable enough to attend playgroups at first, I found myself listening intently to the conversations of other moms and giving out my personal info—email, address, etc.—to be included on information exchanges."

Lisa

So where do you find friends? Oddly enough, I found my first mom friends in a grief group. There were four of us who had suffered the loss of a baby and had attended a couples' course to help us cope with our losses. We each went on to get pregnant in the next year or so, and with those celebrated little miracles, we started getting together every couple of weeks. We went to the zoo together, the museum, and many, many parks. We spent a lot of time in each other's living rooms, watching those kids grow into toddlers and beyond.

You can meet moms in tumbling classes for little ones when your kids can't even roll over yet, the pool, the library, sign language classes, the gym, the pediatrician's office, church, the aisles of a baby megastore, and the crown jewel of many

"The first six weeks you are trying to figure out which way is up. I wasn't getting the warm, snuggly mommy feeling instantly. What saved my life was a 'Help, I Have a Newborn!' class I signed up for through the hospital. There were ten or eleven of us with new babies and a nurse who held our hands and walked us through everything—even how to go out to dinner with a baby. When the six-week class was over, we thought, We can't not have a place to go on Wednesday mornings. So we formed a little playgroup."

Susan

## Playgroups

Make no mistake, playgroups are not always calm affairs! They begin as sweet baby-watching sessions, but as the kids get busier, more mobile, and more messy with a snack, sometimes such gatherings feel like organized chaos. Rest assured, friends and memories last much longer than any mess. Here are some thoughts on productive playgroups.

**Who**: It's helpful to have something in common: children the same ages, same neighborhood, same church, and so on. But open your mind and heart to others. You may want to limit your group to about six children. Too many people might overwhelm your child and undermine your goal of connecting in a real way with other moms. If you create a playgroup of children who live fairly close, they can continue to connect as friends on their own later.

**What**: If you are starting from scratch, talk with the other moms about what you'd like your group to be. Discuss guidelines for siblings attending, sick children, inappropriate behavior, cancellation, and inclement weather. Some groups are very laid-back, while others find success in structure.

**Where**: Trade houses or try new parks. Meet to walk the mall, picnic at the zoo, try the baby pool, or explore a pumpkin patch. Alternate adventures with home meetings, so the process of getting to know each other isn't overshadowed by activities. Create a roster that includes cell phone numbers—great to have when someone runs late or you are trying to find each other at a new venue.

**When**: Midmorning seems to work best for kids and moms alike, but have the foresight to change times if tardiness is a problem or too many naps and feedings seem to be thrown off. Consider whether monthly, biweekly, or weekly fits your schedules and your needs.

**Why**: The purposes of a playgroup should be to give each other a lift, share advice, and engage your children in fun play. Stay away from competition, gossip, and unnecessary drama.

**How**: Rotate hostesses so someone is a point person for each gathering. Be committed if you join, so you don't take a spot that another mom might truly need!

childhoods, the park. Keep a notepad handy in your purse to jot down names and numbers. In this internet age many women can type "playgroup" and the name of their city and come up with a place to start meeting other moms.

"I met a mom who was a friend of a friend. We began to switch kids weekly for three hours to get a little time for ourselves, and we'd walk with the strollers three mornings a week. When I was working so much, it was easy to make excuses for not attending Bible study. She challenged my faith and helped me grow. That was huge."

Kris

My friend Sara took a prenatal/postnatal exercise class when she was pregnant. She chatted up a few women she thought she'd never see again. When she returned with her newborn daughter for another class, she caught up with one mom-to-be from her previous class. They clicked, and much of the class became trusted friends. Together they started a playgroup. Seven years and seven more births later, the playgroup the women started remains connected.

You never know to whom you're talking, whether in a formal setting like a class or casually in a grocery store line. It could be someone you need in your life, or someone who needs you. Don't give up too early on people or activities.

If you are an introvert, it may be difficult to get out as a new mom, let alone strike up conversations with strangers. Structured classes may help you there. Remember, it only takes a small step to get a conversation rolling.

"I love your daughter's shoes. Where did you find those?"
"Are you happy with that stroller?"
"It's nice to get out, isn't it?"

Don't forget neighbors. We were childless and pretty unconnected for years in our neighborhood—garage door up, garage door down at the end of the workday. We didn't even know for weeks that a neighbor two houses down had given birth five days before I did. Having children changed everything. Nearby mom friends are a unique blessing. Walk your

"As a competitive person, it was very hard for me not to compare my children to other people's children. When I started a playgroup, Ben's development lagged behind the other boys. He had trouble communicating, which also made him more unruly than the other children. Honestly, it would make me mad at Ben that he couldn't be like the other boys. Of course I never actually said anything to Ben—he was only about eighteen months old—but I would find myself short-tempered after these playdates. I remember the moms asking if I was worried about him or if I thought about getting him tested. I think it made them feel good about their own children to make me worry about mine. Then I really worried about Ben's speech for the next year and a half until he started preschool when his teachers assured me that he was fine and I had nothing to worry about."

Tracy

neighborhood. You may be surprised at the number of women doing the same.

When you meet women whom you feel a connection to, take the next step and grow that connection. Our group of friends and babies from that grief group became known as "the lunch bunch." We met on Wednesdays at one of our homes, and whoever hosted got the pleasure of a few hours out by herself, while the rest of us caught up and kept up with the kids. And of course, we lunched.

Playgroups, and the more intimate *playdates*, are popular and useful. Women get to connect; babies start to socialize. The information exchange and support can be awesome, as is exposing kids to sharing and to other loving adults. It's also very helpful for your child to learn to nap out of her own crib.

Playgroup dynamics are as varied as the children they gather. Give yourself time to settle in. Give a new group time to find its rhythm, and then assess how it's working for you. Do you look forward to the fellowship? Do you get nervous about your child's behavior? Do you dread the constant comparisons or gossipy atmosphere? Answering such questions about your experience with the playgroup will help you decide if it's right for you.

A friend told me she read about a playgroup in which a woman sharply criticized moms who choose not to breast-feed—as she poured diet soda into her children's sippy cups. Sounds a little extreme, but you get the picture. Follow your values. Follow your heart. Keep your personal priorities intact.

In Terra's first playgroup, she was surrounded by other moms who were fellow therapists and teachers. "I always saw competitiveness between moms regarding whose child sat up first, crawled first, walked first," she said. "One of my friends wouldn't go to playgroup if a certain mother hosted, because she felt like her son was a bully and bad influence.

"You see the same things as your children grow up. I've had parents ask me how my daughter did on her report card. These situations make me think that people are not very confident in their own parenting styles and in their children. It's okay that kids develop differently and have different strengths and weaknesses. It's just not always necessary to point them out to other moms."

Personally, nothing alienates me from a playgroup or any group of women quicker than gossip, whether it's about other moms and other kids, or especially if it's related to male bashing and disrespecting marriage. It's great to have an outlet other than your husband, but friends shouldn't become an outlet for your talking negatively *about* your husband. Another note on dads: it's wonderful if you can connect with mom friends as full families once in a while, so dad can feel

> "I have noticed it takes a lot of trust on my part to allow somebody new into my life. My favorite friendships are the ones where both of us take risks to share deep parts of ourselves and each of us is mature enough to handle it. That's what makes a friendship trustworthy and long-lasting."
>
> Tracy

## Less Time, Same Need

### Finding Mom Friends When You Work

Creating a network of mom friends can be a bit more challenging when you work. You can still take classes, go to the park, rely on your neighborhood, but the reality is that your time for doing so is much more limited. Here are some thoughts from working moms on ways they met and maintained relationships as they went back to the workplace.

**Keep an open mind.** Terra was at a work Christmas party when she was invited to join a playgroup. Karen kicked off a great relationship with another working mom when their kids started babbling to each other in a scrapbook store one Saturday.

**Don't put off meeting other moms.** "I worked with my first child and then quit before my second," Mary said. "But I feel like everybody's already got their groups. I wish I had tried sooner."

**Consider attending new mom classes at the hospital.** They can attract other working moms who are still on maternity leave.

**See your co-workers in a new light**, whatever stage of parenting they may be in. You might find a new friend in an experienced mom who you didn't connect with before you were a mom.

more a part of your daytime world and maybe meet a guy *he'd* like to spend more time with. What a treasure it is to have a whole family your whole family enjoys spending time with!

Having friends who share your parenting style and values becomes more and more important as children get older. First, your time becomes even more precious as your family grows. You simply have less of it to dedicate to friends. Also, discipline may well become a regular feature of your time together, as children test you, as is their job. It's helpful if those with whom you spend time have similar expectations and limits. As you mature as a mom, you will develop a clearer sense of yourself as a parent and a woman. You will know which friends uplift you and your children and which do not.

Finding mom friends is survival. Being one is just as important. You've seen the woman in the grocery store, the

> **Consider joining a local chapter** of Mothers of Preschoolers (MOPS.org) or the La Leche League (Illi.org) that meets in the evenings.
> **Attend a weekend story time** at the public library.
> **Consider online support groups.** "I remember going through periods of devastating loneliness," Ellen said of her days as a new mom and a full-time senior systems engineer. "Online groups helped because they were a way to connect with moms like me that didn't involve having to get my kids packed up and out of the house, go somewhere, spend energy and possibly money I didn't have. I could get online from home while the kids were sleeping. They were a great social outlet as well as excellent for information and ideas." You can chat online or search for a playgroup to attend in person in your town.
> **Network through stay-at-home moms.** Ask them about their working mom friends. Also consider the possibility of a trusted friend who doesn't work as a source of child care. Some stay-at-home moms would welcome the chance to earn money by caring for your child, and you might rest easier knowing your child was in the hands of a friend. A win-win situation for all concerned.
> **Make the most of Sunday mornings.** If you attend church, your child's Sunday school class or a young families class are great places to connect with other parents. If forming a Saturday playgroup sounds appealing, ask your church about posting a notice for interested moms.

one with the screaming child and a full cart. Did you wince? In your mind did you criticize her lack of control? Did you offer encouragement? I think we each have a responsibility to this sisterhood of mothers. At some point, you will be "that woman." How would you want to be treated?

Once I was at a park, chatting with a friend, and another mom was playing with her toddler very nearby. We were in the same general area for an hour before the woman got up the courage to ask me about the church we'd been discussing. She was days new to Colorado, a house full of boxes and a heart full of uncertainty, and here she was prioritizing her child with a picnic and monkey bars. I showered her with information about pediatricians, hair salons, schools, and more parks. I really hope I brightened her day just a tad. She reminded me that you never know where the mom next to you is coming from.

My first playgroup ended gradually, with geography, school schedules, and different lifestyles all coming into play. I still love each woman who was in the group. That we don't meet regularly anymore doesn't diminish what we had or how we helped each other through a formative period in our lives as women and mothers. Change will happen, and we have to let it, whether with our kids or our friends.

## FINDING YOUR MOTHERING STYLE

### Taking Stock

1. How have I seen my relationships change since becoming a mother?
2. Where did many of my current friendships start? What do I value in a girlfriend?
3. What kind of a friend am I? In what ways would I like to improve?
4. In what kinds of settings am I most comfortable meeting people? Am I more social butterfly or hermit crab? How would I like to grow in the area of making friends?
5. What activities appeal to me when it comes to meeting other moms?

# 27

## Keeping Perspective

### *The Woman behind the Mother*

As you cultivate your parenting style and your new community, it's important to remember the *you* beyond the youngsters. There are plenty of pastimes that may have to wait for less busy times, but it's important to find some time for yourself in this era when selflessness is so often required.

My friend Angela went through a time when she felt busy as a mother but lost as a woman. "I realized I didn't have to give all of me up. I had to step back and say just because I'm not working doesn't mean I have to let go of everything

> "Never doubt that a community of thoughtful, committed women, filled with the power and love of God, using gifts they have identified and developed, and pouring passions planted in them by God—never doubt that these women can change the world."
>
> Lynne Hybels, *Nice Girls Don't Change the World*

I was," she said. "You just have to find new niches and support groups that validate what you're doing."

In the early days of mothering, my book group was my special niche. Finishing a novel gave me a rush. Being with women who respected my role as a mom but wanted to talk about much more was very grounding and humbling.

"I still have dreams and desires and aspirations other than motherhood," Barb says. "I feel deprived when those can't move forward as quickly as I'd like. I didn't have the *aha*! moment of finding the perfect career, that thing that propels you before you have kids. So I try to do small things to keep learning and growing."

My friend Sara's mom started an interior decorating business, sewing drapes at home when Sara was young, and later setting up a studio in the basement. Her entrepreneurial spirit, combined with her family-first mantra, was so inbred in Sara that she's done the same, opening a scrapbooking retreat house that allows her to be home with her school-age daughters and husband throughout the week and pursue a business and a passion many weekends.

Some moms just want the opportunity to talk politics, to feel valued as an individual with thoughts and opinions, or to simply spend a day unslimed by a little person. If this is you, you aren't alone. Find a partner and stimulate those brain cells beyond Elmo. Have a grown-up meal with a friend. If

"I have been a self-starter, a dreamer—motivated my whole life. But some of that evaporated in the years after having kids. I knew my husband's and my children's needs, dreams, and desires better than I knew my own. I was helping them to pursue these things while neglecting myself. I began, on some level, to adopt their dreams as my own. Simple indulgences can be satisfying yet hollow, while passion-filled pursuits can bring wholeness and honor over the long haul. It's a process, an awakening, after you have kids."

Kim

"I popped in a CD of all my downloaded business school documents from when I was getting my MBA. I was looking for a marketing plan that I had remembered developing that I thought my husband could possibly utilize with his new business. As I was reading it, I thought, Oh my gosh, I did this. I really am smart! Then I sat and thought how disconnected I felt with who I was then. But as I started to get depressed, I looked at my two-month-old sleeping and popped in on my three-year-old snoring away and I quickly realized I wouldn't trade any of this diaper-changing business for that. I want to use my degree again, but watching Preston giggle yesterday was more exciting than reading that old marketing plan. It's so important for mothers to keep in tune with the fact that they are women too and to keep in tune with what makes them happy when they aren't fussing over their children. You must do something for yourself."

Kelly

you don't desire those things, consider why. It's worth the effort to connect with your God-given dreams because what you have to offer matters profoundly to your family and your community and continues as your children grow. Your goal, after all, is to work yourself out of a job.

I worked so hard at becoming a mom that I was quite content with my new role. I was proud of it and didn't seek a periodic escape like some of my friends. The escapist needs came only after three kids, like my penchant for coffee did. Over the years I've come to see motherhood as not *defining* me but *refining* me. This insight is key to preserving your identity in these early years. You are still who you were before children, but the process of parenting can make you a better woman.

For some women, the thing they do for themselves is simply to do less. "Over time I have come to realize my relationships with other women are far more important to me than a clean house, so sometimes they are invited to join me in my messy house," Julie said.

"Thinning out my schedule was hard for me to do," she added. "When I tell people the limited things I am involved

## Reconnecting with You

Consider your passions, pre-children and now that you are a mom. Do you wish you were still jogging? Still a movie buff? Still interested in that cause overseas? Are there creative ways to pursue those things as a mom?

*Read a book not related to child-rearing.* Even if it takes two months, the satisfaction and stimulation will still be rewarding.

*Try something new.* A recipe, an exercise class, a new way to arrange your living room. Renewal is refreshing.

*Consider waking up in time to do something for yourself before the children rise.* It might be more rewarding than the extra half hour of sleep.

*Journal.* Having an outlet for your ideas and dreams is important, even when day-to-day life may hinder them for a while.

*Have a discussion with your husband about what he thinks your gifts or strengths are.* Are you using them? You might be surprised by the support you get for non-mom activities.

*Assess your use of time.* When you have an hour, are you watching brainless TV? Are you always cleaning? Perhaps you are preventing yourself from having the time to recognize the woman behind the mom.

with, I often get a funny look of disapproval. But it always comes back to 'What is my *end* result?' Now I feel like I can give my best to what I am involved with instead of being involved in many things and really not doing my best. I have learned that saying no is one of the hardest things for me to do, yet I am rewarded every time I find the courage to do so." Your new village—friends or family members—can help you sort through these feelings. Ask a veteran mom, maybe

"I've known moms that can't separate their kids' actions from their own. They take ownership of a fussy day or they apologize for a cranky toddler like they are responsible for his teething. You put undue pressure on your kids and yourself when you do that. Your children don't define you."

Stephanie

someone whose kids have flown the nest, how she preserved the woman inside the mother—maybe even what she would have done differently. You'll be valuing her mothering experience as she helps you plot yours. That's what the village is all about.

## FINDING YOUR MOTHERING STYLE

### Taking Stock

1. Beyond my child, what are my passions and my goals? Is there something I can do in this busy season to further them?
2. What is something new I'd like to try?
3. Do I consider myself a leader or a follower? What qualities in myself would I like to work on?

# 28

## Sitter Savvy

### *Finding Child Care You Trust*

An important aspect of cultivating your new community as a mom is identifying a group of people to whom you can entrust those precious children when you need to be away.

During much of my adolescence, I babysat. I loved the kids, loved the independence and trust I felt, and loved the income. But when it came to getting a sitter for my own kids, I didn't do it. For five years I didn't. I was lucky enough to have my in-laws and a sister living nearby who were willing to babysit, so they were essential to making my extracurricular plans possible.

I was fortunate but silly. As our obligations and desires for grown-up time grew and our need for child care increased beyond what felt comfortable to ask of family, it came time to find a sitter. I was paralyzed by apprehension. Now I had three children under six, including a baby. I'd missed the window for having a teen sitter grow with my kids, and

I had forgotten the trust that was once invested in me as a babysitter.

If I had followed the advice I now hear from other moms, I would have been able to hire a babysitter without stressing over the idea so much.

## Setting Up a Sitter Network

*Cultivate sitters early.* Get to know kids who are approaching babysitting age, so they can get to know your children.

*Ask your friends for referrals of good babysitters.* Sometimes moms are possessive of a favorite babysitter, and who can blame them? But referrals are everything.

*If you live near a university, consider college students,* especially those pursuing a field connected to children. My sister-in-law interviewed college kids, and the one she chose babysat just about every Saturday night for eleven years and even accompanied them occasionally on vacations. They attended her wedding and eventually celebrated the birth of her kids!

*Consider Sunday school teachers or volunteers, or even preschool teachers* as possible sitters, knowing the church or school has already established a level of trust with them.

*Interview your sitter over the phone.* If you are impressed by the interview, arrange a meeting in your home. Watch how she or he interacts with your children.

*Check references.* Always talk to a mom who has used the sitter, asking about punctuality, how he or she handles stress and discipline issues, and how the kids felt about the person.

*Don't always judge a sitter by his or her age.* Many moms find preteens to be more conscientious, have fewer distractions, and express more genuine interest in their kids than do high schoolers. Always speak to the parents

237

**Good to Go?**

It's OK to leave your kids.

You'd probably tell any friend or stranger that. You'd mean it wholeheartedly. So why is it so hard to let that advice soak in when it's you leaving *your* kids?

I could interview a thousand different moms and hear a thousand different stories about how it feels to leave your child in the hands of another. Yours would be different still. As for me, I felt a fair amount of guilt early on. I could be attending a meeting at church, getting my hair highlighted, or going to dinner with my husband—all good causes—and I'd still somehow feel a little "wrong" for leaving my kids with someone else. *Was I too connected to them, too controlling? Did I trust others too little? Did I have a warped sense of how much they needed me—or what I deserved to do outside the home? Did I think I was failing as a mom if I needed time away?* I've come to see I was, and am, pretty normal in my hesitancy to leave.

Guilt is unproductive. I eventually reasoned that you cannot and should not go your child's entire life without leaving them in someone else's hands. So if it had to happen, I wasn't going to make myself miserable each time. I made sure I kept talking to friends who were familiar with the sitter routine and would comfort me or call me silly in proportion to my worries. I was also particular about who kept my kids, so that when I departed I was confident I had done my homework and left my children and their caregiver as prepared as possible.

of any minor you are considering hiring, and ask their opinion of their child's level of responsibility.

*Ask your sitter to take an American Red Cross Babysitter's Training Course and become CPR certified.* Visit redcross.org for more information and classes in your area.

*Try out your sitter for a short time during the day,* or even while you stay at home. Consider popping in to see how things are going when you aren't expected.

*Ask your children (if they can tell you) how the time went,* what they liked, what they played, and what they ate. You never know. One sitter fed my friend's daughter Popsicles and crackers for dinner. She couldn't work the

Also, spelling out to myself what I was doing helped me gain perspective. Was I leaving to indulge in some bad habit? Was I wasting money? Was I seeking to run away from something, like a colicky baby, or running toward something, like a change of scenery or some couple time? It wasn't about right or wrong reasons, but about being thoughtful instead of emotional.

I have several friends who don't think twice about using sitters and grabbing time to sit at a coffee shop alone. I know some feel guilty that they don't feel guilty about leaving! The same exercise in thinking through what you are doing can help put these feelings in proper perspective too.

I realized pretty quickly as a new mom that my baby would pick up on that anxiety. And so do toddlers on up. If I was excited about what I was leaving to do, and the trustworthy person I was leaving them with, there was a chance they would be too. If I cried upon departing, there was a very good chance they would too. I felt I had to rein in my uncertainty for their sakes.

It's healthy for a child to learn to listen to and feel comfortable with other adults. It's great for children to learn mommies have needs too. It may be hard to tell yourself these things with a child crying and clinging to your leg as you try to make it out the door. Is there a worse feeling? But there's another reason to go. Your child will eventually be left at school, or a church nursery, and the sooner they learn that they are safe, and that you will return, the sooner you can enjoy successful and maybe even cheerful farewells.

microwave. Also inquire whether the sitter spent time on the phone or computer.

*Treat sitters with respect.* Have a snack they like and pay them well. Be clear about your expectations. What is intuitive to you might not be to a teenager.

*Extend that respect to payment.* Ask other moms the going rate and make sure you are clear with your sitter on what you pay.

*Don't automatically assume that just because you trust your sitter, you can also trust your sitter's friend.* Your sitter's opinion counts, but you still need to check out the friend before hiring him or her to babysit. You may want to use a team to do the babysitting job. A team has its advantages—more eyes and ears and hands—but if they are more interested in each other than the kids, the team will just be a distraction.

*Consider swapping children with trusted friends.* It's cheaper than hiring a sitter and can lessen your anxiety.

So whom did I find? A friend who knew I was looking for a sitter told me there was an awesome preteen girl who worked in her church nursery. She was so impressed with the girl she started delving deeper on my behalf. Turns out, and this is no joke, she lived on my street. Her mother is a teacher, her father a firefighter. *On my street!* She's the kind of kid who spontaneously creates a volleyball camp for the neighborhood boys and looks out for them whether she's on the clock or not. What a treasure! I only wish I'd found her sooner.

So of course my favorite advice is to look out your window. Know those neighbors. Having a sitter you don't have to transport is not only nice but essential when your husband is out of town and the kids are in bed when you get home from your evening out.

Personally, I'm also a big fan of the family sitting swap. You watch ours; we'll watch yours. I think it's good for dads to see what it takes to take on other children for the sake of safe, reciprocal babysitting. It's cheaper, and your kids get to nurture friendships, you nurture couple friend-

"We went to the local community college and posted an ad at the student center and in the education department with our specifications. This worked wonderfully with us considering most students' flexibility. Another wonderful resource can be the local churches. We have found wonderful babysitters for evenings and summer by asking the girls I volunteer with on Sunday mornings. Most churches do a background check and fingerprint prior to allowing anyone to volunteer, so there is peace of mind that they are prescreened."

Stephanie

"I just love the idea of a babysitting co-op, and it saves me a ton of money. You have to be recommended by a current member, then have your house inspected for safety by one of the officers of the co-op. You pay $30 for coupons and use them to 'pay' other members to watch your kiddos. You earn them back by watching other kids in the co-op. The group members each have two to four children and you earn more 'coupons' the more children you agree to watch. I feel so comfortable with sitters knowing they are other moms who are depending on me too."

Elizabeth

ships, and you help other couples and yourselves nurture your marriages.

However you do it, your "new village" has to include a sitter or two, for sanity's sake.

## FINDING YOUR MOTHERING STYLE

### Taking Stock

1. How do I feel about leaving my child with a babysitter? Do I have a plan for doing so?
2. Does needing time away make me feel like I'm somehow less of a good mom? If so, how can I gain perspective?
3. Do I have a friend or family member I can trust with whom I can trade babysitting? Is there a family that might consider swapping with us on a regular basis?
4. What qualities do my husband and I feel are essential in a sitter? How can I determine if an applicant has these qualities?

# The Bottom Line

*Staying True to You*

I usually attempt to create a Christmas card featuring a photo of my boys. One year I tried several times to get the right picture. First, it was my three boys in handsome sweaters at a community outing. Then they were in Christmas pajamas near our tree. Then they posed at my in-laws' house. I even attempted a bathtub shot. I wanted our friends and family to see the same luminous smiles and radiant blue eyes that I am privileged to gaze at every day. But someone was always too resistant, too tired, or too rambunctious.

One night we began finger painting a birthday card for my boys' Papa. Pretty soon shirts were off and paint was everywhere. Even the baby was getting slimed by his big brothers. I grabbed the camera. Bare-chested and paint-streaked boys weren't the image I had in mind, but the grins were big and the moment was quite reflective of where we were right then: joyful, creative, overwhelmed, and mom outnumbered by four men in the house. We had our card.

Days after the cards were in the mail, I was snapping a picture for something else, and in painless seconds had that "ideal" shot I'd originally been seeking for our Christmas cards. I wanted to jump inside the mailbox and start over. I could practically feel God grinning at a lesson learned, his Spirit reminding me that I can get wrongfully caught up in how the world sees my kids and my mothering. Easy to do, I suppose, with more media messages and how-to books and opportunities for our kids than ever before. We want to do this mom thing right. And it's hard to know what right is.

What really matters is who we are—in the luminous moments and the stinky ones. What matters is how we react to a struggle or a challenge and that we find other women we can share them with.

"You can't be true to who you are if you have to hide it to be in a relationship," my friend Noell said she's learned after ten years of mothering.

"Being authentic is something I've struggled with for many years," Toni said. "I thought if I didn't let people know the real me, it wouldn't hurt as bad when they moved on. But I got to a point in my life when I had lots of surface friendships but no really deep ones. To get to those deep, lifelong friendships meant I had to break down walls and share my true self. This is an area where I hope to teach my children well. I want them to always be who they are, secure in themselves."

In the years to come you will have mommy moments that scar you and scare you, and hopefully you can eventually laugh at them. One day in church I laid my sleeping baby back in his car seat and chose not to interrupt his nap by buckling him in. I covered him with a blanket and carried him upstairs, then downstairs, and finally to the car. I stopped at a grocery store and was walking hurriedly through the parking lot when the seat got instantly lighter. I had unwittingly flopped my three-month-old onto concrete in full view of a bank of pay phones—each one occupied by a man. Mortified doesn't begin to cover how I felt. I didn't put my baby down for six hours.

I also had an elevator door close with my toddler alone inside. My husband let one of our sleeping babies roll off his lap in an airplane, as he too dozed off. Many friends have bumped over their children who have slipped out under the snack tray of their stroller. And I don't know a single mom who hasn't pushed her child's nap schedule to the point of a meltdown at least once.

We all make mistakes. The point is you must give yourself the grace you give your child. You are learning. Don't hide that beautiful process as you seek to form a new community of friends and as you seek to establish your parenting style. You don't know it all, and you never will. You will, though, grow to know your child.

"Seven years and three kids from starting this journey, I am still getting to know who these little people in my house are," Susan says. "I'm still learning to appreciate them."

The same could be said of getting to know yourself as a mom.

"Being 'real' for me is starting with myself," Julie says. "When I am honest with myself first, it is then easier to be honest and real with others. How much can I truly handle this week? What are the important activities for me to accomplish today? What are the end results I want for me, my marriage, and my children?"

It's through that kind of authenticity that we can raise kids to do their best, not pull their hair out at imperfection. It's by being real that we can make friends who enjoy surfing the waves of toddlerhood with us. It's by accepting ourselves and our shortcomings that we can cultivate family relationships that strengthen us, not make us feel small.

Build that village, strong and real. And in turn it will strengthen you.

# Acknowledgments

**From Susan**

Thank you to the dozens of women who shared with me their ups and downs, moments of great triumph and great disgust, and the yearning and yelling in their hearts. You elevate the calling of motherhood by your intense love, dedication, and authenticity.

MOPS has enhanced mothering around the world and now across generations. I am confident, and deeply grateful, that its ripple effects will be felt throughout my family tree. Beth Lagerborg, thank you for asking me to dwell with you in God's perfect timing.

Thank you to Dr. Monica Reed for reviewing this project for medical relevance and accuracy and for her dedication to women's health.

This book was possible because of women I love and was written for women I don't know, including the ones who will one day love my boys. Zach, Luke, and A.J., you are life's most amazing gifts and most humbling projects. Todd, your love inspires me. Our journey with them and with God is transforming my heart. Thank you for never giving up on my becoming a mom.

## From Monica

I would like to acknowledge the team at MOPS International—Mary Beth Lagerborg, Carla Foote, and Jean Blackmer—who extended the opportunity to me to be involved in this wonderful "labor" of love; Lee Hough with Alive Communications—who continues to be an ardent supporter; and last but not least my husband, my children, and my God—all of whom make my life a wonder-filled adventure.

# MOPS

## A Place to Belong

My son was six months old when I attended my first Mothers of Preschoolers meeting. I knew one person in a room of 130. I was clueless about mothering and about MOPS.

Six years later, I can hardly imagine one without the other. I'm a better mother, wife, friend, leader, and Christian for the words I've heard and the women I've met. Sitting with other mothers twice a month simply elevated the calling of motherhood for me. I laughed a lot, made many friends, and deepened my understanding of the privilege and promise it is to be a mom.

> "It's very hard for me to allow someone else to peek behind my curtain. That said, MOPS has really opened my eyes to the fact that women can be real and share without losing face. I have become more compassionate toward others and less judgmental. It's true also for my role as a mother, being better able to extend an umbrella of grace over my children."
>
> Susan

"I think the big turning point in my life was joining a moms group. It saved me, being able to ask, 'Is your kid's poop green too?'"

Elizabeth

MOPS began in 1973 with eight women coming together to talk, eat, share child care expenses, have a craft demonstration, and hear a short devotional. Three decades later this format lives on, with more than 100,000 women served in 4,000 groups—130 of them spread among more than 30 foreign countries. Some groups number just a handful of women; others break 100.

When it comes to creating a network of mom friends, MOPS is a no-brainer.

You might be thinking, *I'm not a joiner* or *I don't like big groups*. Here's the good news for you: MOPS breaks down big groups, and even small ones, into small tables of women who sit together for the year. They eat brunch together, discuss each speaker, plan girl's nights and park dates, celebrate life's highs, and empathize with each other's lows.

I am unabashed in my belief that MOPS changes the world by encouraging moms vocationally and spiritually as they influence the next generation. Here's my husband's opinion: "A hugely impactful thing," he says of MOPS. "I can always tell it's a MOPS Thursday because you've usually been inspired

"After Macie's birth I hit a patch of depression. I had no family near and I knew no one since our move two weeks before her birth. It was all extremely overwhelming. My husband was busy with his new job and meeting new people, but I didn't have the energy or courage to venture out. But I signed up for MOPS, and it was my little light at the end of the tunnel. I met other moms with the same issues—kid struggles, marital strife just after having a baby, total exhaustion. It felt so good to have friends and feel like I belonged. I always felt good walking into MOPS meetings, even after a struggle taking the kids to child care. I finally felt like smiling again."

Stacie

"Whether it's MOPS, or Mom to Mom, or another group, I need that validation and socialization, that sense of purpose. Hardly anyone admits how tough motherhood is. We all know it but we don't say it. It's good to have a place to be honest about it."

Angela

by what you've done, what you've heard, or who you've been with." (He's too private to tell you MOPS has benefited our marriage too, with all the candid speakers on relationships and intimacy.)

Stacia recognizes the same thing: "I joined for selfish reasons—time for me—and it ended up benefiting our whole family," she recalls.

Dana says MOPS impacts her every day. She has a will and her affairs in order thanks to one speaker. She is tremendously cautious about letting her son go to a public restroom alone, thanks to a safety speaker. Her children have chores, thanks to another presentation. And her filing system came as the result of hearing a speaker on organization.

Each of these women represents thousands just like you, who thrive in such an encouraging and empowering environ-

"Before I started MOPS, I had no idea how incredible motherhood and womanhood could be. I was just going through the motions. I thought more about the unnecessary details of mothering than about the really important aspects, like raising my boys to love the Lord and trusting God with their lives. Women can really be incredible to one another. At one time I thought that as a mother I could do nothing for anybody else but my children. When I came to MOPS, women with five children were making each other meals during hard times, watching each other's children, and taking the time to write incredible, uplifting notes to one another. I thought, Wow! I can be more than a mom! MOPS has changed the course of my life completely."

Tracy

"MOPS for me has been a little piece of heaven. Who knew I would find joyin sharing laundry stories and advice on what toilet brush works best? Who knew I would find myself sharing my world with no closed doors? By having an open heart and being authentic, women can really grow and learn from each other."

Hollie

ment. For more information and to find a MOPS group close to you, check out the MOPS website at www.MOPS.org.

**Susan Besze Wallace** was a newspaper reporter for twelve years coast to coast, most recently with the *Denver Post*, before leaving to focus on the daily deadlines of sons Zach, Luke, and A.J. She led one of the largest MOPS (Mothers of Preschoolers) groups in the country and is a contributor to *MOMSense* magazine. Susan and husband Todd recently transplanted their busy brood to northern Virginia, where she continues writing freelance news stories and celebrating the roller coaster of motherhood in print.

**Dr. Monica Reed** is a physician, author, and speaker and has dedicated her life to promoting health, healing, and wellness. She currently serves as CEO of Florida Hospital Celebration Health. Dr. Reed is the author of *Creation Health Breakthrough: 8 Essentials to Revolutionize Your Health Physically, Mentally and Spiritually*. She and her husband Stanton Reed have two daughters: Melanie and Megan.

# Following Jesus Shouldn't Be Just One More Thing to Do

**Jen Hatmaker** delivers forty devotions based on the words and life of Jesus to provide relief for moms of all ages.

Ⓡ Revell
a division of Baker Publishing Group
www.RevellBooks.com